Touched by Tommy

Stories of hope and humour
in the words of men and women
whose lives Tommy Douglas touched

Ed and Pemrose Whelan

Whelan Publications
Regina, Saskatchewan
1990

Canadian Cataloguing in Publication Data

Whelan, Ed, 1919-

Touched by Tommy

ISBN 0-9694622-0-4

1. Douglas, T.C. (Thomas Clement), 1904-   -
Anecdotes. 2. Prime ministers - Saskatchewan -
Anecdotes. 3. Politicians - Canada - Anecdotes.
4. Cooperative Commonwealth Federation - Anecdotes.
5. New Democratic Party - Anecdotes. I. Whelan,
Pemrose, 1919-. II. Title.

FC3525.1.D68W43 1990   971.24/03/092   C90-097157-6
F1072.D68W43 1990

Designed and typeset by **Lazerworks**,
102 McInnis Cres., Regina, Sask. S4R 3E8

Cover illustration by H. Arnold Jacobsen, *Oil Forum*,
April 1954 (SAB: RB-2852)

Cover design by Tim Whelan, Lazerworks

Whelan Publications, Box 31026, Normanview
Postal Outlet, Regina, Sask. S4R 7M0

Printed in Canada by Associated Printers Ltd. 4

Produced with Macintosh® computers

CONTENTS

KEY TO ABBREVIATIONS AND SYMBOLS

CCF	Co-operative Commonwealth Federation	RM	Rural Municipality
NDP	New Democratic Party	SAB	Saskatchewan Archives Board
MLA	Member of the Legislative Assembly	✍	Written contribution
MP	Member of Parliament	☏	Taped interview
		✂	Taken from print source

FOREWORD

Anecdotes are a valuable source of historical truth. Inaccurate in detail they may be, but more often than not they convey an essential fact about a great personage which more formal records ignore. . . .

Paul Johnson

Touched by Tommy is not a biography and it is not a history, though it contains elements of both. Perhaps it is closer to what has become known as oral history. It is based on taped interviews and written accounts, stories of men and women who knew Tommy Douglas, who were his neighbours, worked with him, talked to him, and who were inspired and entertained by him.

Interviews were carried out by several individuals and include excerpts from the series Jean Larmour conducted for the Saskatchewan Archives Board. Written accounts resulted from appeals in *The Commonwealth*, the Manitoba *New Democrat* and to individuals. Another source was print material from columns in newspapers and journals selected to round out our picture of Tommy.

In 1960, Tommy wrote a foreword for *The Compassionate Rebel* by Dorothy G. Steeves. "Today's generation," Tommy said, "needs to know something of the men and women in yesterday's generation . . . learning about the past can equip us to cope with the present and plan for the future." These words have been with us as we chose stories of Tommy when he lived and worked among us.

Tommy retired from active politics in 1979. When asked what he was going to do with his time, he said, in part, "I plan some writing, including a book, I hope, on humour in politics." That book was never written, in good part because Tommy never had the time. His public role continued until shortly before his death.

We hope that some of the things Tommy might have written appear in the following pages. More than anything else they are stories of hope and humour. For those of us who knew Tommy the stories recall the man and his message. For those who did not know Tommy, the stories surely prove that one person can make a difference and one voice can change our world for the better.

ACKNOWLEDGEMENTS

All contributors who helped make possible *Touched by Tommy* are listed in the Appendix. To each we say thank you. We will never forget your interest and assistance.

We are especially grateful to: Eldon Anderson, a stalwart colleague from the day the book was barely an idea; J.A.C. (Jim) Struthers for wise counsel; George Hoffman for his knowledge of the CCF/NDP; Jean Larmour for access to her series of taped interviews as well as her research; Irma Douglas for wholehearted and sensitive encouragement; Gaile Whelan-Enns, Tim Whelan and Debbie Whelan of Lazerworks Desktop Publishing for direction and specific skills in editing and production.

Our debt to the Saskatchewan Archives Board goes back a number of years.

We are also indebted to the authors and historians whose books on Tommy Douglas have been consulted frequently, particularly: Doris French, Dale Lovick, T.H. (Tommy) McLeod and Ian McLeod, and Lewis H. Thomas.

We appreciate the assistance of staff in the offices of the Federal, Alberta, British Columbia and Saskatchewan NDP and the Manitoba *New Democrat*; *Shoal Lake Crossroads*, Shoal Lake, Manitoba; the *Weyburn Review* and the Regina Public Library. We are grateful to the members of the board of the T.C. Douglas Calvary Centre for their hospitality and co-operation.

Thank you to each contributor who lent us personal photos and clippings, and to Bruce Westin, Dixie Photo Services, Regina.

All contributions, written and spoken, will be deposited with the Saskatchewan Archives to augment sources regarding Tommy Douglas and the Co-operative Commonwealth Federation/New Democratic Party.

Ed and Pemrose Whelan
Regina, Saskatchewan
September 1990

Dedicated to

Irma Dempsey Douglas

. . . Irma was always there with a cheerful word,
no matter how black things were, . . .
The darker it got the more cheerful she was.

Tommy Douglas, Nanaimo, 1976

◆ 1 ◆

The Manitoba Years ◆ 1911-1930

Tommy was 20 when he enrolled at Brandon College, Manitoba. With his mother and sister Nan, he had arrived in Winnipeg, then a city of 150,000, in 1911. Tom, his father, had come out the previous year. It was a 17 day boat trip, delayed by fog and ice, and a five day train journey from their home in Falkirk, Scotland.

Tommy Douglas was born on October 20, 1904, christened Thomas Clement Douglas. He was Thomas for the long line of Douglas sons with that name, and Clement for his mother's family. His younger sister, Isobel, was born in Winnipeg in 1911. That year Tommy was operated on for osteomyelitis; trouble with his right leg would be intermittent for the rest of his life. This experience was the beginning of Tommy's commitment to universal, public health care.

In 1919 the Douglas family came to Winnipeg for the second time. They had returned to Glasgow, Scotland when Tom, Sr. enlisted in World War I. Tommy attended school and worked at a variety of jobs.

Back in Winnipeg, Tommy began his apprenticeship in the printing trade. At Beulah Baptist Church there were activities almost every night, and three services on Sunday. At 18, Tommy was in demand as a lay preacher. In this period he took up boxing and was twice Manitoba lightweight champion.

He was active in Scouts and DeMolay, took training in public speaking and gave recitations at concerts.

Yet in a number of ways life in Falkirk and in Winnipeg was similar, centred on family, church and work. The political struggle in Scotland—the world of Bobbie Burns and Keir Hardie—was replayed in Winnipeg. Tommy was part of the working class north end which would send J.S. Woodsworth and Stanley Knowles to the House of Commons.

Tommy said that J.S. Woodsworth and printer friends influenced his decision to continue his education. Brandon College had about 200 in attendance including students from Weyburn, Saskatchewan. In his six years there he took high school, then Arts. At college Tommy took elocution classes, was active in drama, debating, sports and in student organization.

Students who would become ministers spent weekends and the summer months in rural churches.

T.C. Douglas as a student at Brandon College, 1924.

For Tommy these were Austin, Carberry, Shoal Lake and Strathclair, Manitoba. It was at Carberry in a Presbyterian church that Tommy met Irma Dempsey. Later, she attended Brandon College to study piano.

Towards the end of his college days Tommy and fellow student Stanley Knowles went to Calvary Baptist Church, Weyburn on alternate Sundays. The congregation chose Tommy, while Stanley went to a Winnipeg church.

Men and women who have memories of Tommy as student minister have contributed the following anecdotes.

TOMMY AT SHOAL LAKE

Shoal Lake Baptist Church, where Tommy was minister in 1929, as it is today.

I was in my early teens at the time when the student pastors from Brandon College came to the Shoal Lake and Strathclair Baptist Churches.

My parents, Angus and Jennette McBain, were stolid Baptists. Fundamental I suppose one would call them.

My dad, a deacon, taught the Bible Class for many years and mother played the organ in our little church. Thus it was a natural that the student pastors would come to our home to stay over and preach on Sunday afternoon.

Mr. Douglas drove a coupe (make unknown) and travelled around a lot to the separate homes to visit. He was very popular especially among the young people.

My parents respected him, but my dad did not always agree with his ideas on social customs.

I remember that his sermons were always just 20 minutes long. I don't ever recall him using a note.

He liked to use a soloist for his service to reinforce his text or theme.

He was a great leader of the BYPU (Baptist Young People's Union). Young people between ages of 14-21 came from all the churches in town. He used a brand of discipline that had them all respecting and liking him. I remember those meetings so well, the religious part as well as the wiener roasts in summer, sleigh rides out to farm homes and snowshoe parties in winter, all such good, clean fun.

I also recall his fiance', Irma Dempsey from Carberry, coming up from Brandon College with him on the odd Sunday, a pretty, petite brown-haired girl sitting demurely in the back seat of the church. (I had heard it said that the girl he married would have to be pretty.)

During his service he always had a message for the children, which delighted them, also he would teach them a little song once in a while. One I remember was, "I've got the joy, joy, joy, joy down in my heart, down in my heart, down in my heart to stay."

His sermons were always so interesting. No one would fall asleep. One in particular was his Christmas message, "The Fourth Wise Man." It was in the form of dramatization and he took the part of the fourth wise man. It was so well done that after all these years it is well remembered.

At the Baptist Sunday School picnic out at a farm home—McFadyn's—on a very hot day, I was back-catching for a ball game and got too much sun. After it was all over, I took quite ill. Mr. Douglas was staying at our place and recognized it immediately as sun stroke. He knew what to do, ice packs on the back of my neck and head. He told my parents that he would sit by my bedside until he was sure I was going to be all right. I have never forgotten his care and thoughtfulness at that time.

✍ **Eva Mundell**

T.C. Douglas while a student minister at the Carberry, Manitoba, Presbyterian Church, 1927.

vice in the evening. If it rained in the summer, the Kippen car would have difficulty at times in getting Mr. Douglas to Shoal Lake and back. They would have to get out and put chains on the old Model-T Ford car. In the winter, no matter how cold and stormy, the Kippens would take Tommy by team and cutter.

At that time my Dad had a contract to drive a school van. The route went through the Kippen yard. We would pick Mr. Douglas up on Monday morning in the van, take him to the station to meet the 9:45 am train back to Brandon. We all would look forward to Monday morning, as Mr. Douglas would entertain us until we arrived at the station. I well remember him telling us of his experiences as a boxer and how to deliver that knock-out punch.

✍ **Kenneth Rapley**

STRATHCLAIR-SHOAL LAKE

Tommy Douglas was a student minister at the Baptist Church on the Strathclair-Shoal Lake field during 1929-1930. At that time he was a student at Brandon College. He would take the train from Brandon to Minnedosa, change trains and arrive in Strathclair on the 3:45 pm train.

He stayed with the Kippen family, two sisters and two brothers, who were in their sixties at that time. They lived one and a half miles west of town, near the railway track. When no one was there to meet him, Tommy would walk down the track to the Kippen home.

On Sunday, the Shoal Lake service was held in the afternoon and the Strathclair ser-

THE KID PREACHER

In later years Tommy loved to tell about the Sunday morning he arrived in Stonewall, Manitoba. . . . He was only 18 but looked much younger. . . . The whole congregation—about 40 persons—came down to the train station to meet the visiting preacher, but nobody noticed him.

Tommy, seeing a young boy standing alone beside the station, asked as quietly as possible, "Where's the Baptist church?" The boy, looking surprised, said, "Are you the new preacher?" "Yes, I am," replied Tommy.

Then, in a voice you could hear from one end of the platform to the other, the boy shouted, "Ma, this kid says he's the preacher."

✂ **Jean Margaret Crowe**

Two Sermons

I was 13 or 14 when Tommy Douglas took the Sunday services at our church in Shoal Lake. He was someone you didn't forget.

One sermon I remember was in the Christmas season, about the Fourth Wise Man. He told it in the first person: he had started out with the other three wise men to follow the star in the east, but turned back and returned to his home.

Before his sermon he always had a story for the young children, usually with an object to demonstrate his theme, such as a rusty old nail or an apple with a worm in it. The children enjoyed these stories and listened closely.

During the war, my friend and I heard that Tommy Douglas was going to take the service at the Broadway Baptist Church in Winnipeg one Sunday, so we went to hear him.

When he got up to give his sermon, he took out his watch and placed it on the altar and said it reminded him of a story. Two neighbour women, one Catholic and one Baptist, agreed to go to each other's church for a Sunday service.

They went to the Catholic church first and the Catholic woman explained everything about the service to her friend.

The next Sunday they went to the Baptist church and when the minister got up to speak he put his watch on the altar and the Catholic woman said to her friend, "What does that mean?"

Her friend replied, "It doesn't mean a thing."

✍ **Mrs. H. Lindsay**

Tommy Douglas while a student.

Tommy's Flair

I remember Tommy Douglas as a young, enthusiastic minister at the Baptist Church in Shoal Lake, Manitoba.

He was an excellent speaker and had a flair for holding one's interest. He gave little talks to the Sunday School classes prior to his sermon. I remember vividly a lesson on The Heart. He flashed a lovely, clean, red heart, then told what happened if we strayed, lied or stole. He said some magic words and presto— a big, coal black heart replaced the red one!

He wrote in my autograph book:
Sept. 29, 1929:
Dear Wilma,
If instead of giving gems or flowers, we could drop a beautiful thought into the heart of a friend, that would be giving as the angels give.
T. C. Douglas.

✍ **Mrs. Wilma Hatch**

ELOCUTIONIST

Tommy was a trained elocutionist. He had taken it at Brandon when he was a student. He started with no high school, so he had to do his high school which took three years, to get his college entrance, then three years university; so he was there six years. All the "theologs" were required to take this course in elocution, one of the things that explains why the Baptist preachers largely are better speakers than anybody else. Tommy was very active in theatricals, and he did a lot of readings.

As a matter of fact, when he was at Weyburn for the last couple of years, until he became active in politics and had to give this up, he was giving elocution lessons himself, putting on recitals. He was, in short, a "ham." This was all part of the trade as far as he was concerned. He was an actor.

Ⓞ **T.H. (Tommy) McLeod**

BRANDON DEBATING TEAM

Well, Tommy was always a charismatic sort of person. He was very boyish looking when he was young, but always exciting in ways of expressing himself. I think, perhaps, he became noted very quickly as a speaker. Before he was at Brandon College a year he was a member of the debating team. We had a debating team that won a number of contests, they even defeated the Oxford Debating Team from England, Tommy and a fellow named Fred Friend.

Tommy Douglas and Irma Dempsey on their wedding day in Brandon, 1930.

Friend was a great digger for facts and figures and Tommy was a great person to sum up everything and they made a really good team. That would be in 1925 or 1926.

Ⓞ **Rev. Armand D. Stade**

◆ 2 ◆

The Weyburn Years ◆ 1930-1944

The year 1930 was eventful for Tommy. He was ordained in June at Calvary Baptist Church, Weyburn, and married in August at Brandon with Stanley Knowles as best man.

Tommy and Irma lived in Weyburn during the years of drought and depression, years of need and hardship for a great many families whose courage and resourcefulness were remarkable. George Anderson of Cadillac, Saskatchewan, put it in these words: *Use it up. Wear it out. Make it do. Or, do without.*

Government measures, private charity and individual initiative were not enough. People like Tommy and some of his neighbours decided to strike out in a different direction. Tommy was active in forming the Weyburn Association of the Independent Labour Party (ILP). The Saskatchewan ILP joined the United Farmers of Canada (Saskatchewan Section) to become the Farmer-Labour Party, playing a key role in the 1932 Calgary convention where the CCF was born.

In 1934, Tommy ran for the Farmer-Labour Party in the provincial election. In 1935 he was elected as CCF Member of Parliament and began 25 years as representative for Weyburn, both federally and provincially.

In 1944 he took his seat in the Saskatchewan Legislature and became Premier on June 15, four months before his 40th birthday.

A New Pianist

One Sunday, Tommy said, "Next Sunday we're going to have a new pianist." That's when he got married. The next Sunday Mrs. Douglas came. And that added quite a bit to the service.

✤ **Don Goranson**

A Saskatchewan farm yard during the 1930s.

Down to Earth

Tommy taught elocution and stage techniques. He taught us how to project our voice. He taught us never to turn our backs on the audience and not to look directly at the audience. He taught us how to speak and how to stand correctly. These were the same techniques he used when he spoke.

I had a part in a play that Tommy directed. It was a comedy called *Old Crusty Takes the Air*. Tommy was the main character—Old Crusty.

His involvement in drama and elocution was uncommon for a minister but the community seemed to accept it. Whatever Tommy did drew a crowd. Practicing was great fun. Both he and Irma were so hospitable and filled with fun. What I remember most is how much fun it was. You never felt in awe of Tommy. You felt that he was one of you. You never felt that because he was a minister he was above you. He was down to earth.

✤ **Babs Robertson**

White Gift Pageants

The White Gift Pageants were really the talk of the country. People came from all around. It was just like a great big play. We put it on in the church which was very small quarters for that. We had committees for wiring and for the costumes.

Everybody had a costume, the Wise Men, shepherds, Baby Jesus, angels. Mrs. Douglas and I were usually in charge of the music and we were behind the scenes. They moved the piano into the back room because they needed all the space for the stage. This was a major production and I can remember a couple of times Tommy put on plays in one of the halls too. It was all church youth who took part. That was another way of helping the young people, giving them something to do, because this was one of Tommy's major interests.

✤ **Helen Davidson**

IN THE DEPRESSION

I think that the young people especially were impressed by the fact that in a time of need, in the Depression, the first thing he thought about was to have people working so that they had enough food and clothing. We also knew when these big packages came from the East. There were even trunks, and everything else, clothing, barrels of apples and food and all sorts of things came from Ontario. And I think the people began to look to him to help them.

✺ **Helen Davidson**

TOMMY AS FIVE YEAR OLD

My first experience with Tommy Douglas was at a concert in South Weyburn School about 1931. Tommy got on the stage and acted the part of a five-year old reciting the poem, *Twinkle, Twinkle, Little Star*. He got off to a good start, then he started to stutter, presently he was crying, then he would wipe his nose with his sleeve, and then he ran off the stage.

✺ **R.A. Cugnet**

YOUNG PEOPLE'S SERIES
CALVARY BAPTIST CHURCH
WEYBURN, SASK.

At 7 p.m. on the following Sundays:

May   4 -- *What is Life ?*
"   11 -- *"Mother."*
"   18 -- *Choosing Your Life Work.*
"   25 -- *Imagination — Your Master or Servant ?*
June 1 -- *Your Body and How to Control it.*
"   8 -- *Life's Crossroads.*

Come and hear a young man deal with young people's problems.

WE INVITE YOU

T. C. DOUGLAS

Weyburn Calvary Baptist Church sermon schedule for T.C. Douglas' young people's series.

RIDE FROM THE POLLS

My brother, Bill, and I were threshing at Ogema when the 1944 election took place. Mrs. Leah Brock, my mother, notified some party members that we were available to vote so a driver came and picked us up and took us to Weyburn. We voted and then hadn't any way back to our job, so we phoned the headquarters.

In the meantime, Mr. Douglas had won his seat.

About midnight, Mr. Douglas and Jack Powers came and took us back to Ogema. We realized in later years very few in his position would have done this.

✐ **Brandon (Bud) Brock**

BOYS' GROUP

It was about 1932 when I started high school that I became involved with Tommy, chiefly through his boys' work in conjunction with the three churches, Baptist, United and Presbyterian. There was a very happy relationship between the three pastors of these churches, and one of the common ventures was this boys' group that Tommy headed up.

It was simply a boys' program, bearing in mind that these were the depression days and young people didn't have too many outlets for their energy.

Co-operative Commonwealth Youth Movement Hallowe'en party, Weyburn, 1945.

We had two evenings a week, one of which was devoted to all kinds of athletic ventures,- basketball, baseball, boxing,- and one evening was devoted to discussion and study.

We called him Mr. Douglas. In his own way he was one of the gang but, at the same time, there was no question that he was the leader of the enterprise and respected by all the boys.

Personally, he had a tremendous impact upon me. I saw a great deal of him, quite apart from the boys' work. I got into the habit of dropping into his study at the church and talking to him. And he was instrumental in my going to Brandon College, his old college.

✥ **T.H. (Tommy) McLeod**

WHAT HE PREACHED

In Norway from the age of 14, my father, Axel Hansen, was on his own and worked as a man. He was exploited and cheated by a so-called religious relative, so he grew up with a very low opinion of preachers.

He moved to Minnesota when he was 17, and had a similar experience which reaffirmed his lack of respect for preachers.

My father later farmed in the Weyburn area, and during the drought, when nothing grew but Russian thistles, he couldn't find feed for his horses and cattle. The benevolent government offered to buy cattle at a cent a pound. My father refused to sell at that price and, instead, butchered and took the meat to Weyburn to give it away to the unemployed.

That day, he met a young preacher named Tommy Douglas who was very active in helping the unemployed people and who arranged for the distribution of the meat.

I still remember my father coming home, full of enthusiasm because he had met a preacher "who was trying to practice what he preached." Dad became one of the early members of the CCF and campaigned vigorously for Douglas and the CCF to the end of his days.

✍ **Esther Hansen Mackey**

PUPILS AND PROGRAMS

Mr. Douglas had a large library of books. He believed in teaching us a variety of readings. Some were humourous, others witty, some sad and others happy. He taught us to do imitations,-take one person's part when we were saying what they said, and take the other person's part when they spoke.

Besides the individual pupils, Mr. Douglas had classes with both men and women. He trained us in impromptu talks, to take opposite sides in debates and rebuttals.

On Sunday nights after church sometimes Mr. Douglas would have his pupils put on a recital in the Baptist Church. Some would give readings, others play the organ, piano or violin. Mr. Douglas himself would give some readings. At the end we had a cup of tea, a sandwich and a cookie, and real good fellowship.

In the fall of the year, they had country fowl suppers. Mr. Douglas would take his car, and he and Irma would take two or three of his pupils to take part in the program. He never missed an opportunity to give his pupils a chance to do their part.

✪ **Christena Fox**

YOUNG LIBERAL

We came to Weyburn in 1927. When I went to collegiate in McTaggart, our teacher encouraged me to take part in oratorical contests. When Mr. Douglas came I asked if I could take lessons. He was such an outgoing person that it didn't take that long to get known in the community.

I wasn't a Baptist, I was a Presbyterian and still am. In those times there were both the Liberals and Conservatives. I was very much on the Liberal side, from my upbringing. I really wasn't involved in anything other than his elocution class. Of course it didn't take me too many times listening to his beliefs and speeches to know his ideas and ideals were what I believed in.

✪ **Christena Fox**

A NEW BABY

I heard a neighbour, a good friend of ours, telling my dad about a young man saying that he had gone to Tommy Douglas. And he said, "My wife and I expect a baby; we have no money; we have no clothes for it and we just don't know what we are going to do."

In a short time, that couple received a parcel which included baby clothes and everything that would be needed for a newborn infant. And so, as the story goes, the young husband went back to Tommy and told him— there was no name on the parcel—he told him that they received this parcel. And he asked, "Where did it come from? Did you have anything to do with it?" And Tommy said, "Was it all right?" And the fellow said, "It was just great." "Then that's all that is necessary," said Tommy, "don't think anything about it."

✪ **Lorraine Butters Boyle**

Douglas is On !

Tears are not far away as I remember my experience as a child of the 1930s in southwest Saskatchewan, known then as the heart of the dust bowl. One of my most poignant memories of the 1930s and the new challenge of the 1940s centres on one man who gave us poor farm families hope.

That man was Thomas Clement Douglas. He was a voice of reason and caring, when all else about was deprivation and discouragement. Weather had dealt farmers a serious blow, and many were cultivating what nature meant to be grassland, but a greater factor was tired, insensitive and corrupt government at the provincial and national levels. They simply weren't dealing with the problem.

In the 1930s, Douglas spoke out, advocating needed change, sometimes in Parliament, sometimes from the pulpit, and always as a responsible citizen dealing with the immediate problem of real human beings.

In the 1940s he acted, as Premier of Saskatchewan, to effect the much needed changes he had so eloquently advocated.

When I was a child, travel was difficult because of distance and the fact that most families didn't have a car. Some didn't have money to buy gas for their vehicles. We relied heavily on radio to get our information. It possessed immediacy along with emotion and humanity to augment a couple of conservative farm journals.

The radio star was Douglas. When he spoke, my mother went to the door of our tiny house and yelled across the farmyard, at the top of her well developed lungs, "Douglas is on." Regardless of what was being done, it stopped, and my father, sometimes a hired man and I would hurry to the house. After listening intently, often with an ear to the old Philco because the battery pack wasn't always replaced on time, we'd have coffee and a doughnut and return to work. We were truly refreshed. The grain may not have been coming as it should, the crop may have faltered, and it appeared Sonny couldn't go to Normal School this fall, but we sensed some purpose in keeping on. Our faith in the future and, even more so, in ourselves, was at least momentarily restored because someone with power and credibility knew and cared.

The only other message I now recall my mother sending across our farmyard with great volume was, "Check the lease fence because the bull's gone again."

When Douglas spoke and later acted, there was no "bull." He'd experienced adversity in an economic system stacked against working people. We believed in him, and followed him out of the considerable depth of the Great Depression, to a caring, sharing, co-operative and virtually self-sufficient province.

We owe him a great debt. My mother was right. Douglas was "on."

✍ **Eldon Anderson**

Where it Hurts

About 1941, Tommy was speaking down at Wood Mountain and we went to hear him. After we sang *O Canada*, he sat down—the chair gave way and he fell off the stage, his feet up in the air. When he got up he was rubbing himself and he said, "That's just where Jimmy Gardiner gives me a pain."

✦ **R.A. (Bob) Walker**

Tommy Douglas, candidate photo, 1935.

CHICAGO SHANTY TOWN

Prior to becoming Premier of Saskatchewan, Tommy was a close friend of a number of members of the Wilcox United Church.

Although this denomination was not Tommy's personal choice, he was prevailed upon to take anniversary services at the United Church at Wilcox for several years.

Tommy, as everyone who knew him would remember, always recounted at least one of his numerous experiences along with the sermon.

One I remember well took place during his university life in Chicago. He, along with several other university students, had heard about the deplorable conditions which existed on the river banks outside the city. They formed a small group to go down to the river and see for themselves what things were like. They were warned it was a dangerous undertaking and that someone could be seriously hurt and perhaps killed by the 'Bos (hobos) as they were called.

These young students refused to be discouraged and one evening visited the cardboard Shanty Town which was considered by all citizens, police included, to be out-of-bounds.

As they prowled through the filth and degradation, a miserable occupant emerged from one of the shacks demanding to know who they were and what they were doing there. Tommy stepped forward explaining they were university students and was there anything they could do to improve the plight of the man and his friends. The man's answer was:

"No! young man, there is nothing you can do for us. You and your friends go back to university, get an education and change conditions so that future generations will not have to exist as those of us here are doing."

Tommy hesitated for what seemed like a full minute. He then leaned over the pulpit and told a full church of his solemn resolve to do everything within his power to follow the advice of the hobo in the Chicago Shanty Town.

✍ **Gareld K. Clements**

"We must settle down to a lower standard of living." E.J. Young. (Hansard, Feb. 9, 1933.)

mrs T.C. Doug

Children Come First

VOTE FOR DOUGLAS

Blotter from the 1935 federal campaign when Tommy was first elected to the House of Commons.

Tommy's Commandment

The first time I ever heard Tommy Douglas speak was at a Sports Day in Ratcliffe. I was a teenager, and not interested in politics, but Tommy kept everyone listening. In fact, the farmers, old overalls patched and repatched, were laughing with tears running down their faces—laughing for the first time in years. They were enthralled with Tommy's ideas and were completely won over by Tommy's commandment that the poor should have as much chance as the rich, and every man was his brother's keeper.

✍ **Veronica Eddy Brock**

Tommy Was a Leader

We put on a meeting in Davin School, Regina. It was in the early 1930s. Tommy Douglas came. I happened to be chairman. I was amazed when he came. He was so vital, definitely poor, and I didn't know what I was going to hear. But when Tommy began to talk, you could see he had the crowd enthralled. Me, too. An amazing man. He stood above us all and we knew right then that Tommy was a leader.

✆ **Russell McKenzie**

CAR TROUBLE

One time he had a political meeting at Schneider School, nine miles northeast of Weyburn. After the meeting Tommy's car wouldn't go. So he came over to our place. Tommy knew nothing about cars. My brother and I pulled the car with a team of horses until finally it went. He visited Mom and Dad in the house until we got the car going.

He had meetings all over—in schools and halls. Sometimes there was a big crowd and sometimes only ten people. Tommy seemed satisfied with just ten people. People went to listen to him even if they didn't agree politically. He was interesting, sharp. He knew the people's situation and what their needs were.

During one campaign he had a meeting in Weyburn. There was a big crowd and Tommy was an hour late. Finally, he came. He had driven from Montmartre and a wheel on his car had fallen off. Tommy was fiery mad. The wheel nuts had been loosened and he blamed it on the Opposition.

✦ **Roy Coleman**

FARMER-LABOUR CANDIDATE

Tommy ran for the first time in the provincial election of 1934 in the Weyburn riding. He was a candidate for the Farmer-Labour Party. Dr. Eaglesham won. Afterwards Tommy said, "Anybody who hasn't any more friends than I have in this town should carry two guns."

✦ **Hugh Alexander**

Election piece used in 1935 federal campaign.

HUMANITY FIRST !   DEMOCRACY NOW!!   JUSTICE EVER!!

THE C.C.F. WILL PROTECT OUR HOMES, OUR RIGHTS, AND HUMAN LIVES.
Other parties will protect the multi-millionaire and plunge us into war.

NOW IS THE TIME

Vote for your wife and little children. : Vote for yourself and the common people.

Now is our chance.   Think carefully.
This is your day..   Vote wisely.

VOTE DOUGLAS

For Prosperity, Peace and Security.

COURTESY OF

E. CRANDELL
FLOUR AND COAL

Office 97.. .. Phone.. .. House 79

RADVILLE, SASK.

DOUGLAS
The youthful, smiling exponent of justice, freedom and fairness.

J. S WOODSWORTH
The loving, striving, sacrificing champion of Life and Humanity.

GRANDMA'S HELP

In 1934 when Tommy Douglas first ran for public office he was opposed by Dr. Eaglesham, our family doctor in Weyburn. Tommy was concerned about how he could get people south of Weyburn to vote for him. I said, "Let me try it on Grandmother."

I mentioned to Grandmother what I thought was my best point, that Tommy Douglas was a minister of the gospel, and that he'd be an excellent man to vote for. Grandmother agreed with this, but she found it difficult to not vote for the family doctor.

When the relatives from the south came into town they always came to Grandmother's for a noon lunch. They'd ask her, "How are you going to vote?"

She said, "You're going to vote for Mr. Douglas."

"Well, why him?"

"He's a minister, and you're going to vote for him."

Well, I guess she must have convinced them, because that was a solid block for the CCF from then on.

✍ **Roy Borrowman**

THE CO-OP REFINERY

Harry Fowler and other co-op leaders told the story of one incident in the early days of the Co-op Refinery, and how the co-ops came to rely on Tommy Douglas to do battle for them.

Co-op people laboriously got together $32,000 to start building the world's first Co-op Refinery in Regina in 1932.

In May 1936 the Ways and Means Committee of the House of Commons reported on proposed amendments to the Customs Tariff, in connection with the budget of the Liberal government of the day.

One item was of great concern to the young Co-op Refinery which imported light crude from Kalaspell, Montana, free of duty.

The government proposed a new duty of half a cent per gallon on the light crude.

In the House of Commons on May 20th, Tommy moved, seconded by M.J. Coldwell, that the item be restored to the former level, but was ruled out of order.

In the debate Tommy described the change from horses to tractors on prairie farms and the economic discrimination that led to the Co-op Refinery.

Condemning the new duty proposed by the government, Tommy said, "It would look to many as though the voice may be the voice of the government but the hand is the hand of the large oil concerns."

Tommy's shrewd comment hit the mark. He was quoted again and again in co-op meetings. The version I heard went like this: "The government may have written the amendment, but the hand that guided the pen was the hand of Imperial Oil!"

This was the beginning of Tommy's association with the co-ops and their commitment to him, according to the co-op leaders of the day.

✍ **Ed Whelan**

RETURNING AS MP

Tommy would come tearing in the back room where the choir congregated and the very first thing as he popped in the door he just picked me up in his arms and kissed me and that would be the end of it. We exchanged greetings and so forth. When he got into the church and after he had been introduced and before he started on his discourse, he would say how glad he was to be back. He would say, "I think I am really unique. I think I am the only minister in the whole of Canada who can come back to the Baptist church and kiss the organist. I am the only one this ever happens to."

The place would be packed when he came back. There was rarely room for everybody. Other congregations, when they heard he was coming back, would share the service with us. It was always a big drawing card to have Tommy come back as guest speaker. Perhaps he enjoyed the time downstairs even more than he did the service, because at the service he had to be the main speaker. When he was downstairs he let his hair down and had a visit with everybody.

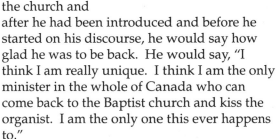 **Helen Davidson**

Weyburn Baptist Church where T.C. Douglas preached from 1930 to 1935.

GOPHER TAILS

I recall in the election in 1934, Tommy came to Wynyard to speak. He pulled a gopher tail out of his pocket, saying we could get two cents each, and that for 20 gopher tails we could get half a pound of tobacco. I smoked a pipe then and the Chateau tobacco from Quebec wasn't all that good.

This story has stayed with me because it tells how hard up we were and that Tommy wanted to do something about it.

✍ **Chris Schubert**

TOMMY VISITS ODESSA

I met Tommy Douglas for the first time in 1941. He was the federal MP for Weyburn and my home town of Odessa was in the Weyburn constituency. Tom Runge, one of the original CCF members in the Odessa district, brought him to our house. (Tom Runge was perhaps one of five people who voted CCF in the early 1940s.)

Odessa was a very Catholic area and, at that particular time, people were under the impression that the CCF Party was anti-religious, anti-Catholic. In fact, Tommy Douglas once quipped, "See, I'm in power and I haven't closed up the churches." So Tom Runge's idea was to garner more Catholic support for Mr. Douglas, and he felt that dad, because of his past experience with corrupt Liberal administrations, was ripe to convert to the CCF. So he brought Tommy Douglas to our farm.

We had a very old house. We had no electricity. It was evening. We were sitting in the kitchen, that was the usual meeting place. I was a lad of ten and I was expected to go to bed rather early. But I was curious about the discussion that was taking place and I sort of stayed in the background and listened to Mr. Douglas talk in a very friendly way to my father, trying to convince him of the merits of the CCF program. And also trying to dispel any prejudice that could have existed regarding Mr. Douglas and the Catholic Church.

I was very taken up with this man and I dare say that, in later years, I came to like him because of that initial experience.

He listened to my father tell him of how debt ridden we were. Our farm was mortgaged and we had paid the banks many times over. And dad thought that was grossly unfair. Dad hadn't the title to his land. Mr. Douglas promised that when he was in a position to do so, he would resolve that particular situation. And, as we know, in 1944 one of the first things Mr. Douglas did was to bring in the Farm Security Act.

I realized that Mr. Douglas was a man of his word, that he was a man of integrity and, above all, he was a man who went to bat for the little people.

⚙ **Fr. Isidore Gorski**

CONFUSE THE ENEMY

In 1941, Tommy and I, along with older professional men around Weyburn, joined the 2nd Battalion of the South Saskatchewan Regiment. Tommy wanted to go on active service but he was rejected on medical grounds. While training at Dundurn, where Tommy and I occupied the same tent, we were subjected to lectures by noncommissioned officers who, in many cases, were not qualified nor were they knowledgeable. In one instance we went to a certain hut for our morning lecture only to be told that we had to go to another hut. When we returned to that hut for our afternoon lecture we were advised to go to a different hut. The "witty" sergeant told us we were being moved from hut to hut to confuse the enemy. Tommy Douglas, in an audible whisper, remarked, "Why don't you have him attend the lectures?"

✍ **Roy Borrowman**

IN THE RACKET

It was the fall of 1943 when I first saw and heard Tommy Douglas. We lived on a farm near Prince, 15 miles north of North Battleford. In church on Sunday morning at the end of his sermon, Rev. George Connelly announced that Tommy Douglas would be speaking that coming week in Meota, six miles north of where we lived.

Because harvest was over and my parents were anxious to hear more about the CCF and the bright young leader, Tommy Douglas, we got into our 1929 Plymouth and drove to Meota. The hall was packed. I remember the enthusiastic clapping when the chairman announced, "Tommy Douglas, the next Premier of Saskatchewan." He soon had people in peals of laughter. One joke remains in my mind.

There were two cats watching a tennis match. One cat was watching every move. His eyes were fixed on the ball as it went back and forth, back and forth. The other cat, who wasn't really watching the game, tried to get the cat, watching the game, to talk.

"Hi," he said. The first cat said nothing.

"Hi," he said again. "Why are you watching the game so intently?"

The cat with his eyes on the game finally said, "Well, you see, my old man is in the racket."

Tommy went on to relate how bankers, finance companies and big business people were in the racket to keep the poor farmers and others paying the piper.

✍ **Peggy Durant**

Shirley and Irma Douglas in Ottawa, 1936.

PHEASANT SUPPER

In 1943 at Lake Alma, dad came home one night and he had guests with him, one was Ed Stinson and the other was Tommy Douglas. There was no cafe in the town and dad asked mother if she would get some extra food for these two gentlemen. My mother went downstairs and came up with a can of pheasant. Dad was a good hunter and mum canned it in sealers. She warmed it over in the frying pan with the potatoes and corn. For years and years after, Tommy reminded her of the pheasant supper he had with us.

⚘ **Stan Oxelgren**

DEMOCRACY BREATHES

I must record T.C.'s visit to the Turtleford constituency in November 1943 in preparation for the 1944 election. I recall one of Tommy's remarks while we drove along, "I will drive as long as I can keep a tire on my car." It was late in the fall and cold. I had borrowed my brother-in-law's old vintage Chevie sedan, no heater, drafty doors and dangerously apt to break down. My one sole aim was to get to Pierceland and back without mishap to men or car. Tommy was not dressed for a trip in such weather so we got him into one of Bill Schwandt's old fur coats on top of Tommy's dress coat, put a blanket around his knees and feet and away we went. Not once did T.C. Douglas complain.

We called at St. Walburg, Barthel, Loon Lake, Goodsoil and Pierceland, meeting with people at the back of stores or poolrooms. Only in Pierceland did we have a hall and a well organized meeting with a reasonably good turnout.

I have never ceased to be amazed at taking a speaker of Tommy's calibre on such a trip with so few in attendance. We had to rely on notification by mail and hope for the best. It was 125 miles from home to Pierceland. Tommy treated everyone we met as very important. In other words, he made Democracy the living, breathing thing it is supposed to be.

✍ **R.H. (Bob) Wooff**

UNOFFICIAL PASSENGER

In May 1944, I had been a flying instructor for a year at the RCAF Service Flying School, Yorkton, Saskatchewan. Occasionally when we had no other duties, instructors would fly aircraft for overhaul to the Repair Depot at Moose Jaw. One very hot afternoon that May, I was asked to take an aircraft down for a major overhaul and was informed that I would have an "unofficial" passenger. Being a New Zealander, at the time I had no idea who my passenger was. His name does not appear in my log book, but it was T.C. Douglas campaigning for the memorable June 1944 provincial election.

I was fascinated to listen to Tommy's vision of Saskatchewan's future. I was so absorbed that my navigation was only incidental, resulting in having to land at Swift Current instead of Moose Jaw. The unusual heat of the day was creating severe thermals and thunderheads and we were heavily buffeted all the way. While we were being viciously thrown against our harness as the aircraft thrashed about, T.C. kept talking and I, as a backsliding Presbyterian, was thankful that I had a Baptist preacher along. We landed "roughly" at Moose Jaw; I was exhausted while T.C. was still unflappable.

Now, 45 years later, that hour with Tommy is still one of the greatest experiences of my life, the most unusual hitch-hiker I ever met.

✍ **Ian J. Wilson**

A Better World

I must go back to when I first knew him . . . in the 1930s. It was a risky business in the 1930s to be associated with such a movement as the CCF. He laid his career and his livelihood on the line. His courage put courage in others. His belief in people gave people faith in themselves that they could together improve their conditions. His passion for social righteousness lifted their hearts and roused them to joint action.

What I remember most from those dozens of meetings in his office (when he was Premier) is his unfailing cheerfulness. Because he quoted them so often I'm sure he believed Robert Burns' words that "A time is coming when man to man the world o'er shall brothers be for all that."

When I was most downhearted he would quote me a line from Tennyson, slightly amended: "Courage my friends, 'tis not too late to make a better world."

✂ **Carlyle King**

Tommy Douglas with members of his congregation in Weyburn, spring 1930. Back row, left to right: Harley Shaw, M.F. Brown, Dan Sinclair, Aaron McKague, Ted Stinson, Mrs. Dan Sinclair, Tom Earl. Middle row: Mrs. Mary Orth, Mr. Royce, Nurse Royce (Miss), Mrs. W.H. Shaw, unknown. Front: Mrs. Norman McKinnon, Mrs. Jimmie Dickson, Iris Bean, Mrs. Pettis, and Rev. T.C. Douglas.

Weyburn in the 1930s.

WEYBURN YOUNG PEOPLE

I was teaching the kids at school, and he had them in his church, so we had quite a bit in common. On Sunday afternoons we met to hold discussion groups, Tommy and myself and a number of other young people. We discussed the local social problems, and national and international problems. And of course, at that age, we pretty well had most of the answers.

It was Tommy's idea we have discussions. I think partly the reason was that he was rather unhappy about the number of young people wandering around Weyburn who had nothing to do. Many were unemployed.

We put on plays. Tommy had experience in acting, so he would do the directing and I would promote these plays and manage them. We had a lot of fun with this kind of thing.

✍ **Roy Borrowman**

TOMMY AT GLENARCHY

My first meeting with T.C. Douglas was in the fall of 1935 when Tommy was speaking in our country school, Glenarchy. I was unable to attend as our twin daughters were then less than one year old. About 9:30 pm my husband called and asked if we could put up a couple of fellows for the night. Yes, we could. The two fellows were Tommy Douglas and a Mr. Emery from Assiniboia. What a privilege and honour to have had Tommy Douglas in our home!

I have heard Tommy quote, "Without vision the people perish." *Proverbs 29:18*.

✍ **Mrs. Elizabeth Little**

◆ 3 ◆

The Saskatchewan Years ◆ 1944-1961

Tommy and Irma and their daughters, Shirley and Joan, lived at 217 Angus Crescent, just south of College Avenue and west of Albert Street. Tommy frequently walked to the Legislature, south across Wascana Lake on the Albert Street Bridge, and then east to the Legislative Building.

The family belonged to First Baptist Church on Victoria Avenue. Shirley attended Davin School and Central Collegiate, Joan attended Davin and Luther College. In summer, time was spent at their cottage on Carlyle Lake.

In the years 1944 to 1961, Tommy Douglas and the CCF won five successive June elections. Saskatchewan was transformed.

This chapter describes Tommy Douglas as premier, cabinet minister, administrator and Party leader. We see him in one-to-one situations and at crowded meetings throughout the province, in Caucus with the MLAs and in the Provincial Council of the Party.

Anecdotes are presented under six headings:

Tommy: One to One
Platform Magic
Tommy and the CCF Party
Tommy and the MLAs

A CCF Government:
    Civil Service and Administration
Humanity First: CCF Programs

Tommy: One to One

ALWAYS ACCESSIBLE

I grew up in a Liberal household. I never understood then, and still don't, how the Liberals managed to convince many of their less sophisticated adherents that T.C. was slippery and not trustworthy.

I was surprised, therefore, to find that T.C. was a warm, plain, sympathetic and principled man. I remember standing behind him in the Legislative cafeteria one lunchtime and watch him order what was then his standard lunch: poached eggs on toast, buttermilk and stewed prunes.

I knew that I could often get him on the phone in the morning between 8:30 and 9:00. He was always accessible to the reporters from *The Leader-Post* (Regina), in part because he was like that and in part, I suspect, because he knew that he could easily neutralize the Ted Davis/D.B. Rogers editorials by cultivating the reporters. Most of us quickly grew to be sympathetic, because we liked Douglas and because our mentor, Chris Higginbotham, shaped a lot of young minds.

✍ **John Schreiner**

(Note: C.H. (Chris) Higginbotham was author of "Off the Record: The CCF in Saskatchewan" (1968). His series of interviews taped in 1958 were the basis for "The Making of a Socialist: The Recollections of T.C. Douglas" (1982) edited by Lewis H. Thomas.)

HE MADE TIME FOR PEOPLE

When my wife died after five years suffering from cancer, Tommy came out of a cabinet meeting to come to our house and offer condolences.

He had the ability to make time for people; ability to make decisions. Regardless of the problem, one could present it to him and get a decision. Suggestions regarding policy in a few words. Guidance for solving that particular problem and for weeks and months ahead.

It was not necessary to camp on his doorstep; he had time not only for me but for everybody.

⚗ **B.N. (Barney) Arnason**

HE KNOWS HOW TO FIGHT

I remember Tommy coming in to the Laird Gymnasium, Regina, one day and he really shook them up. I looked up and here he had a guy, showing him, "Get your hands out there." The fellow who ran the gymnasium was standing there watching. And everyone said, "He's the Premier!" They all came running, these kids. "He knows how to fight," one kid said. "Tommy showed me how to fight."

⚗ **Percy Brown**

ICE CREAM CONES

This Tommy Douglas story came to me from the late Joe Ward of Tompkins, Saskatchewan.

It was a Sunday morning in the early 1950s. Joe Ward was in Regina and being a charter member of the CCF he wished to call on his idol, Tommy Douglas.

Tommy's wife, Irma, said the premier wasn't at home, that he was taking the children from Dales House (a foster home for boys) out for a walk.

Joe decided to drive around the area, certain he could not miss Tommy with a little army of boys in tow.

Sure enough, along College Avenue, Joe spotted the group, all the boys licking ice cream cones. Behind them walked Tommy, his famous smile lighting his face.

✍ **Luetta Trehas**

A GOOD LIBERAL

When I had my lawsuit, I had the lawyer from Kamsack, and he was a staunch Liberal, is still a Liberal. We went to see if we could get some help at the Legislature. I can remember well how he said: "You know I am not a supporter, but I've got to give T.C. Douglas credit. Since they got in I can come in the front door without a cheque in my hand. When the Liberals were in, you couldn't come in the front door, you had to go to the side door." And that was the word out of a good Liberal.

⚘ **R.A. Cugnet**

Clarence Fines and Tommy Douglas at a picnic for a group of U.S. co-operators, Legislative Grounds, Regina, August 1946.

OPEN DOOR POLICY

There were hundreds of farmers coming who wanted to talk to Tommy and he had an open door policy. Our office was full of people all of the time. And he sat back just as cheerful and relaxed as if there was just one man in the world, the man he was talking to, and he had lots of time.

We did have to screen people a bit, but if he were free, he was always willing to see people—especially if they had a problem. We tried to handle as many of them as we could, or refer them to another minister, if it was something to do with another department.

The phone just rang about every five minutes. We tried to get them to make an appointment if it was someone we knew he would like to see. We never let anybody with a problem go.

⚘ **Eleanor McKinnon**

Tommy Douglas visits Saskatoon Light Infantry-Machine Gun, First Canadian Division, Holland, 1945. Patch reads: "Sask. L.I.-M.G.-Canada." (Saskatoon Light Infantry-Machine Gun).

nately, I am very much better, and I sang my first performance last week in Munich. Mrs. Spry so kindly called me from London, and we have made the necessary arrangements."
SAB **Douglas Papers**

WORLD WAR II

One thing that comes to mind is during the war, when Tommy went Overseas. Bill, my husband, showed him around the area where the Canadian troops were stationed. Bill was in London at Canadian Military Headquarters.

Tommy had an appointment with some one important for dinner at the Savoy. Bill didn't know this and asked Tommy to come up to his place and they would find something to eat. And Tommy turned down the important invitation for a little chat and dinner with my husband. Bill had been Overseas over five and a half years. It was natural for Tommy when he was going over that he would say he would look Bill up, and it just happened that Bill was given the job of taking him around. Bill and I really appreciated that Tommy gave me a full report.

✸ **Eva Bethel**

HELP TO EUROPE

Irene Salemka, former Weyburn resident, wrote to Mr. Douglas from Frankfurt, Germany on November 6, 1959. She had been in a car accident and in hospital for several months, unable to work.

As a foreigner, she could not borrow money in Germany. She needed $1,500 to tide her over until she could work again. She asked Tommy if he could put her in touch with a loan company in Regina.

Tommy had been in Europe himself. On his return he instructed her by telegram December 4, 1959, to phone collect Irene Spry, wife of the Saskatchewan Agent General in London.

Irene Salemka wrote on December 9, 1959: "I can't tell you how much I appreciate your help at a time when I most needed it. Fortu-

Tommy Douglas presents awards to Regina Little Theatre players at Dominion Drama Festival, 1948. Bill Walker is recipient.

FRIEND OF LITTLE THEATRE

I knew Tommy in another role, as a father, because my wife, Helen, was very active in Regina Little Theatre and Helen played along with Shirley Douglas in a number of productions. Tommy was a great supporter of Shirley and of the Theatre and would always ask me how Helen was, because Helen and Shirley had gone to St. John, New Brunswick where their play won some awards. He had a real interest in what Shirley was doing and he related to other people in the cast.

✐ **George R. Bothwell**

PLAYING "O CANADA"

I think it must have been in the late 1950s that Tommy came out to a political meeting in Colgate. As quite often happened, I was called to the platform to play *O Canada*. After we had the singing of it and I got up to go back to my seat, Tommy came to me and said, "That was *O Canada* played as it should be played."

That made my day. I felt quite honoured.

✐ **Lorraine Butters Boyle**

CAN WE BE OF ANY HELP?

About 1945 with my parents, Roy and Irene Vanstone of Lang, Saskatchewan, I was motoring to Regina on an August morning. Car trouble forced us to stop at the roadside.

While waiting for assistance, a black limousine-type car came by and stopped just in front of us. Immediately, the right hand back door of the black car opened and out stepped a man who briskly moved toward the stalled car. My father recognized the good samaritan, and said, "Why, that's Tommy Douglas."

Douglas went to the driver's window and said, "Hello, can we be of any help to you?" On learning that help was on the way Douglas left, as courteously and sprightly as he'd come.

This experience confirmed our belief that Douglas was a practical, caring man who not only believed that people came first but also practiced it, even when serving as Premier of the Province.

✐ **Jean Anderson**

Tommy Douglas, Mrs. Eva Phelps and Joe Phelps at Pionera, Saskatoon during the 50th Anniversary celebrations in Saskatchewan, July 1955.

ONLY ONE TOMMY

The first time I heard Tommy Douglas was at Hafford during the 1944 election campaign. My brother and I went to hear him. And from the first day I laid my eyes on him I fell—almost—in love with him, and our relationship and friendship lasted all the days of his life.

From then on there was only one political party for me for the rest of my life, and it was really due to my attending that first meeting with Tommy.

Walter E. Smishek

BOUNTIFUL MEAL

I recall one occasion in the 1960s when my husband and I attended a political meeting in Glaslyn, Saskatchewan accompanied by our teenage son. The main speaker was Tommy Douglas. We were always enlightened by his down-to-earth speeches, and enjoyed his jokes and stories. A bountiful meal had been served and at the close, Tommy, as was his custom walked among the crowd shaking hands and chatting. We were among those to greet Tommy; he placed his hand on our son's shoulder. Later I remember saying to Gordon, "I guess you won't wash that shoulder for a while, eh?"

Evelyn Sannerud

ENCOURAGEMENT

I think he was interested in Colvin, my husband, because he was impressed by the fact of someone leaving their country and coming to better themselves in Canada, a positive thing about Colvin, that he had left Trinidad to come to Canada. Tommy always said hello to Colvin.

Tommy wanted to know what Colvin was doing, and Colvin told him he was in a psychiatric nurse training program at the Saskatchewan Hospital in Weyburn. As time went on, Colvin felt that he needed to go further and he kept in touch with Tommy, and Tommy would always ask what his future plans were. Colvin said he wanted to go to university and get a degree. Whenever Tommy saw him, he would ask for a progress report.

Colin worked as instructor and supervisor at Weyburn.

He went on to an M.A. in psychology and worked as a clinical psychologist with the Regina Mental Health Clinic, and consultant with the Regina Police Force for 19 years and with the RCMP, and was guest lecturer at the Canadian Police College in Ottawa.

Colvin died suddenly in December 1987.

I always felt that the encouragement Tommy Douglas gave Colvin and Tommy's interest in Colvin's work over the years really meant a great deal to Colvin.

⚲ **Elsa Peyson**

AT CARLYLE LAKE

Things were very informal at the Lake. One thing, although we were together a lot during the week, I always stayed away on weekends because Tommy would come home; he would be tired and I felt that he deserved time to himself. But they used to drop in every once in a while.

The first time I ever read an Agatha Christie book was one I borrowed from Tommy. I remember thinking at the time, someone like that reading an Agatha Christie book. I realized afterwards that he needed the relaxation. He used to always bring bread from Regina, National Bakery bread, because the bread was different. In spite of all the problems he had, he would go right down town and pick up a few loaves of bread and bring it down to the Lake for us. It was marvellous.

⚲ **Eva Bethel**

TRUSTING YOUR PREMIER

They respected Tommy in the rural areas and they believed him. And that is still true. Even kids that were mere children at that time still have that great feeling that Tommy was the man to believe, and the man to lead, the man who did things for them.

This of course was Tommy's forte. Tommy was one of those who had the uncanny ability to remember these people and call them by name. Those people felt that Tommy was their friend and that they could totally trust him. And I believe they got that feeling because Tommy was never manipulative. Tommy was definitely honest.

⚲ **Eiling Kramer**

HUNTING SEASON

I was assigned to the North Battleford territory as co-operative management advisor, Department of Co-operation and Co-operative Development, when the Hon. Tommy Douglas was the minister. The year was in 1951 in October and hunting season was open. The Department had developed a new business survey program in order to try to assist retail co-operatives.

On the Monday morning the research economist and I were to start out about 8:00. On reaching the car I noticed a special looking case in the back seat and asked, "Who plays the clarinet?" The economist said, "Well, I do; bring your saxophone," which I did.

Completing our day's work at the co-op and having had our evening meal, I suggested that we play a tune. I was very disappointed to learn that the case in question contained a shotgun, the economist being a duck hunter! We didn't play.

Subsequently at a staff conference, I related my experience about this trip and the shotgun. Tommy Douglas smilingly remarked, "I can think of no better accompaniment for a saxophone than a shotgun."

✎ **Lloyd Lokken**

Tommy Douglas speaking on Co-op Day, Regina, August 24, 1951.

DEAR LEWIE

Thanks very much for your letter of April 30 and for sending me a copy of the letter you mailed out to a number of newspapers, regarding the recent oil deal.

In my opinion, the private oil companies were very ill advised to stir up this hornet's nest. They have been treated exceedingly well by the Government. I think it's time somebody told the public, as you did, of the squeeze which was put on the co-operatives during the war, in an attempt to deny them crude oil supplies.

Now with reference to yourself, before you start to raise hell with anybody else, you'd better listen to your doctor, because I am certainly on his side. Please make up your mind that your first job is to get well and not to worry about the co-ops or anything else. So just relax and devote some of your energy to convalescing and keeping your blood pressure at a normal level. If I hear any more nonsense about your carrying on a lot of correspondence from your bed, I am going to have you transferred to the psychiatric ward and put in a straight jacket. This is my final warning!

SAB **Douglas Papers**

(Note: Lewis L. (Lewie) Lloyd (1898-1987), long-time co-op leader, was special assistant to the Premier in the Department of Co-ops.)

Daughter Shirley Douglas examines Tommy's headdress after he has been named Chief Red Eagle of the Assiniboine tribe at Piapot Reserve in Saskatchewan, July 1945.

FARMERS TRUSTED HIM

Tommy wasn't a farmer, he didn't know too much about the everyday operation of a farm. It showed up very quickly that he wasn't a farmer, when he talked to farmers. And he wasn't the kind of person to try and imitate the farmer. A farmer is a very skeptical individual. Nobody can spot a phoney faster than a farm audience. Tommy never tried to be anything that he wasn't. And the farmers trusted him.

✍ **Don Sinclair**

THE PREMIER AND KIDS

There were always children at CCF and NDP meetings, conventions, socials, and fundraisers. And Tommy Douglas would often direct part of his speech to us. He always assumed there were children present and he treated children as individuals with the directness that was his style.

It felt like he remembered being a child, knew what we were feeling, especially at functions in the adult world. Frequently I would find myself registering the Premier, or delivering a message before a rally. Always I was treated as an equal with the assumption that I was an integral part of the event.

It is the opening ceremonies of the Legislature that stand out in my memory. Lined up with the Cabinet and Caucus, family members and children were part of the ceremonial procession. Tommy always put us at ease, asked about school, told us a story if the strain of waiting showed.

All was done with acceptance, not adult to child, but person to person. He always remembered our names. I often imagined him as my peer, ten years old playing baseball, sitting in class writing a tough test, square dancing during phys. ed. What a wonderful classmate he would have been. Having him at school would have put to rest the politics of the playground, I had no doubt of that!

While giving the province courage and its people their self esteem back, Tommy was a friend and an example to the children who knew him.

✍ **Gaile Whelan-Enns**

Courtesy & Humour

During the provincial election of 1960, a rally was held at the Sharpe Auditorium in North Battleford.

Ted Boden and I arrived early, but the auditorium was filling up very quickly. There were a few seats available around the entrance when Tommy came in. After shaking hands with everyone within reach, he sat down to await the call to arms. He did not remain seated long as he saw a lady standing, and he promptly found her a seat—his own, and he stood in line with many others along the wall.

Tommy said that he and his driver had taken the opportunity to drive through the grounds of the Provincial Hospital. They were impressed with the lovely lawns, well trimmed hedges, and with the beautiful flowers. They stopped to admire them and noticed a fellow standing alone close by, and went over to speak to him.

I extended my hand, said Tommy, and said, "How are you, sir, and what is your name?"

The fellow said, "Oh, fine, my name is Bob". Then, after a pause, he said, "Well, who are you?"

Tommy Douglas addresses a Physical Fitness Banquet in 1945. Woodrow Lloyd sits to the left of Tommy.

Tommy said, "Oh, I'm Tommy Douglas. You know, the Premier of Saskatchewan."

"Ho, ho. You'll soon get over that. When I came in here I thought I was Napoleon."

✍ **Chris and Jeanne Delahoy**

The Crusaders

At First Baptist Church in Regina, Tommy had a boys' study group known as the Crusaders. He not only conducted the study group but took them for outings. He took a personal interest in our son Morley and each of the boys; a personal interest was typical of his attitude toward young people generally.

✍ **B.N. (Barney) Arnason**

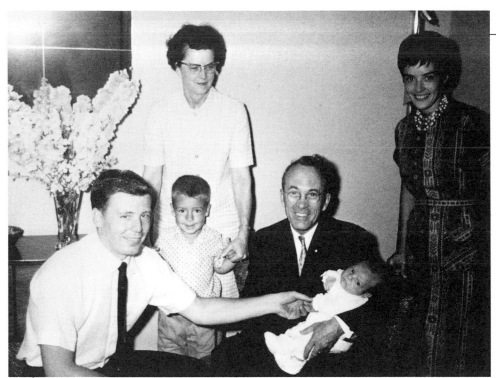

John Brockelbank, son Greg with Irma Douglas, and namesake Douglas being held by Tommy Douglas. Ina Brockelbank on the right.

NAMESAKE

When our second son was born, June 15, 1963, we named him Douglas, after Tommy. We have a picture of Tommy holding our Douglas when he was about six weeks old.

About 17 years later, at the opening of Tommy Douglas House in Regina we told Tommy that we would like to recreate the happy moment of 17 years earlier in a picture again. Tommy took a look at our Douglas, now 6′2″ tall, and said he would just as soon stand beside him as hold him!

✍ **John E. Brockelbank**

PRIME MINISTER AND PREMIER

. . . Had a pleasant talk with Douglas, new Premier of Saskatchewan, who called with his Minister of Finance. . . . I confess I was very pleased to see Douglas looking so young and enthusiastic about his work, and a young man with him as Minister of Finance. It recalled my early days in government and I spent some time talking to the two of them about their opportunities, the pleasure it gave me to see them taking on new responsibilities, wishing them well, though regretting the defeat of the Liberals. Told them I expected them to win; the previous government had made a mistake in extending its time. . . .

✂ **Mackenzie King Diaries**

(Note: The Minister of Finance was Hon. C.M. Fines. Mackenzie King refers to the June 15, 1944 Saskatchewan election, "the defeat of the Liberals.")

FATHER OF DAUGHTERS

I concluded my elementary school education in the late 1940s and early 1950s at Davin School, Regina. Tommy's daughter, Joan, and I were classmates.

One evening in the spring of grade 5 or grade 6 two other young boys and I were in the neighborhood of the Douglas home and

Shirley Douglas and father Tommy pumping water, 1944, at Carlyle Lake.

decided that we would call on Joan to see if she could come out.

We obviously made so much noise that we were heard within the home, the front light went on, the door opened, and there was Mr. Douglas. We were extremely uncomfortable and this must have been obvious because Mr. Douglas descended the steps and came over to us on the lawn. He asked each of us our names and why we were there. When we told him that we had come to see if Joan could come out, he said that, no, she couldn't since it was now getting on in the evening and, in any event, he did not appreciate the fact that we had been hanging around outside his home for no apparent good reason. He did add, however, that on another occasion, if one or more of us wished to come and ring his door bell, as he expected proper young boys to do, he would consider whether that occasion would be appropriate for Joan to go out.

I was shattered. I was certain that I would never be forgiven. On reflection, Tommy probably went back into the house and chuckled.

A few months later, I was standing with a group of other children on the Albert Street Bridge, watching a cavalcade of cars drive by. Mr. Douglas, passenger in the back seat of a convertible passing by at a relatively slow rate, picked me out of the crowd, called my name and waved and smiled to me.

It was a significant moment to me, and one which endeared him to me forever.

✍ **Harvey G. Walker**

CABINET KIDS

He was very good with young people. He used to be just like one of the family, as far as I was concerned. We'd get into these little jousting matches, and all of a sudden, he'd take me down and pin me. He was a powerful little guy.

I think he was good with all of the cabinet ministers' children—any of them that I knew all considered Tommy to be their friend. And he called all of the children by name, and knew every one of them, and seemed to be sincerely concerned about how we were doing. He had a soft spot for young people.

He would show up at Co-operative Commonwealth Youth Movement meetings. Being a young person at the time, I was impressed by that, and found that, in the future I could phone his office, at any time, and get right through.

✍ **Murray Fines**

Tommy Douglas makes a presentation of cameras to the Richardson Brothers, Canadian and international curling champions. Left to right: skip Ernie, third Arnold, second Garnet, lead Wes; Saskatchewan Legislature, March 1960.

WOULD YOU LIKE A RIDE?

In the late 1940s, a friend and I were leaving the Legislative Building one evening after having concluded some business about our hospital with the Health Department.

As we came down the steps Tommy passed the time of day with us and then asked if we would like a ride down town. As we were travelling on the bus we gladly accepted. We felt highly honoured. I wonder how many times the Premier of Saskatchewan has made an offer of this kind.

✍ **M.E. Cottrill**

Platform Magic

THAT VOICE

The things that man could do with words. I've read about all these people, Disraeli and all the others who were supposed to be able to mesmerize a crowd.

One election, in particular, I remember driving up to little northern schools and places up there, the other side of Kelvington, Spalding and Naicam.

These halls were full. I never got over the thrill, because I was sitting up on the stage where you could see all the people. You wouldn't even think they were listening. They'd be sitting there and then finally a face would lighten up and somebody would laugh. He'd tell them a few stories. He'd have them laughing and he'd slowly work into the meat of his speech. And they'd start shaking their heads. He'd be telling them what was wrong, how they were being robbed and what we had to do. He'd get near the end of his speech and that voice of his would take on a kind of a timbre, you know. And they applauded and cheered.

✍ **Percy Brown**

HOME FROM THE WAR

I had just come home from Overseas to find my wife deeply involved in political organization. She had been with Louise Lucas (organizer and gifted orator active in the farm movement and CCF) during her last illness and was inspired by her dedication and self-lessness. A convention was coming up and she wanted me to go with her. I demurred as I felt that I would know no one there and having been away for four years was woefully out of touch with public life. I was not certain that I even wanted to become involved. And so it was with real reluctance that I walked into the hall with Olive that night feeling very much a stranger and out of place in a hall full of civilians.

Suddenly Tommy Douglas came out of the crowd, his hand extended and a genuine smile of welcome on his face. "Welcome home, Carl, we're glad you're back safely, you fellows did a fine job over there." He remembered my name from Olive speaking of me, he remembered where I'd been and he cared enough to single me out of a crowd. And so when I think of Tommy Douglas, I think of his genuine caring and his love and concern for individuals and the endless hours of labour he expended for his fellow men.

✍ **Carl N. Wells**

Tommy Douglas addressing Regina Labour Council, 1949. Ed Whelan, Council secretary (left), T.C. Douglas, Harry Chappell, Howard Conquergood (behind microphone), Pemrose Whelan, alderman L. McK. Robinson.

ELEPHANT AND THE CHICKENS

I remember the first joke I heard Tommy tell, about the elephant and the chickens. The punch line was: "Everyone for himself," said the elephant as he danced among the chickens!

✿ **Elsa Peyson**

IMAGE OF TRUST

He was what he was supposed to be. That is, his image was the kind that people would like to have it be. He was an image of trust, integrity, courage, a moral voice, and above all, perhaps, the humanity and understanding element coming through it all. And, of course, a person with authority, without a "pushy" presence at any time. He obviously understood people very well. I think Tommy knew very quickly the people in the audience that he was addressing. He was an amazing man in that respect.

✿ **W.G. (Bill) Davies**

EARLY DEBATES ON RADIO

The beginning of my being influenced by Douglas was in the formative years when I was a boy, when Dad and I listened to the radio debates from the Legislature. Immediately the nature of his message, the passion, the commitment for the ordinary guy, the sincerity, the humour, the philosophy, young as I was, had a very big impact on me.

✿ **Roy Romanow**

LOCAL CALL

In Minneapolis in the 1950s at a conference of the Co-operative League of the U.S.A., Tommy gave one of his famous jokes that went the rounds and was repeated again and again.

It was about a Texan, big, loud, vociferous, wealthy with many business interests, who had also attended a conference in Minneapolis.

He phoned from his room, then went downstairs to the telephone operator.

"Can you help me with this call? I want to call Midland, Texas."

"Certainly, sir."

The lines were busy. Finally the operator managed to get through. The Texan talked for about three hours, then asked, "What's my bill?"

"It's $56.24, sir."

The Texan was indignant. "Why, in Texas, I could call clear to hell and back for $56!"

"In Texas that would be a local call, sir," replied the operator.

⊗ **Marvin Bix**

Tommy Douglas talking on a rural wall phone (Assiniboia . . . Weyburn 1944 Directory).

This Man Tommy

I met Tommy Douglas for the first time in 1957. It was at a meeting in Weyburn. I don't remember where it was but it was a big meeting and everyone was all excited about this man Tommy. I didn't know who he was, but when I saw him I realized why they were all excited. He was dynamic.

His concern for people impressed me, that everyone should live a good life and not lack the essentials, things he considered essential, health, education.

After I knew Tommy Douglas, I always felt that I couldn't think of just myself, I had to think about other people and their welfare.

He was Premier of the Province and he could have just sat back and enjoyed being Premier of the Province, but that wasn't enough for him. He had to make sure that everyone else had the same choices in life. Once you listened to him and observed the way he lived, there was no way you could have thought otherwise.

⊛ **Elsa Peyson**

In Our Own Hands

Premier Douglas addressed a capacity audience which time after time cheered him to the rafters. "No Moses will come out of the wilderness and open up a Utopia for the common man. Our fate is in our own hands. If we are united, we can march forward together to the new life. Salvation for the common people will come by our standing, working and fighting together."

✂ **The Manitoba** *Commonwealth*

Tommy, Irma Douglas and Bill Surdia, June 15, 1954, on 10th Anniversary of the election of the CCF in Saskatchewan.

Tommy on the Radio

My experience in politics began probably from age 15 when I travelled with my father to town and he would carry on the fight, with the CCF message, in a very Catholic community.

When the radio broadcasts were carried from the Legislature, and even before that, whenever Tommy Douglas was on the radio, I would rush in from wherever I was, because I knew Tommy was going to be speaking.

Later on when I became a school teacher, I couldn't very well listen to the broadcast from the Legislature in the daytime at school. I would listen to the rebroadcast at midnight.

⊛ **John R. Kowalchuk**

Tommy Douglas opening a bowling tournament for provincial civil servants at the Bolodrome in Regina, 1952.

with his stories and laughing at his jokes, thoroughly enjoying the whole speech. Our plans of playing hooky were completely forgotten, and not one of us mentioned how hard the seats were getting.

✍ **Freda K. Longman**

TEACHERS IN-SERVICE

There were 600 of us from the Yorkton-Melville superintendency who met at Foam Lake in 1948. There wasn't a sound in the hall except Tommy speaking upon the atrocities committed at Belsen and Buchenwald and all the other concentration camps. He explained it in sad and torturous language, and the hard evidence that was still there, when Tommy and the rest of the Canadian politicians had gone, I think it was in 1945 or 1946, to these places.

Tommy made a terrific impact no matter what the political philosophy of the teachers there; I think there wasn't one person who walked out of that hall without the deepest appreciation of the message that Tommy had brought to us. It was really evident how effective the man was.

⚙ **John R. Kowalchuk**

TALKING TO TEENAGERS

I attended Regina Normal School. As part of our Social Studies we were allowed to attend speeches by politicians and, this time, Tommy Douglas was speaking at the Darke Hall on the campus. Off we went to what we thought would be another boring afternoon with seats getting harder by the minute. On the way over some of my classmates decided that we would sit in the back row, where it wouldn't be too noticeable to slip out the door, and go down town to browse in the stores.

Well, Tommy started speaking, and to this day I am amazed at how he held the attention of a bunch of teenagers. We sat enthralled

TOMMY AND HECKLERS

I remember a meeting when former Liberal MLA Hubert Staines heckled Tommy. There was a three-party discussion on wheat. Walter Tucker (Liberal) was there and Alvin Hamilton (leader of the Conservatives).

Somebody asked Tommy a question. Hubert Staines said, "Mr. Chairman, is Mr. Douglas answering the question or is he making a speech?"

Tommy stopped short and said, "Frankly, Mr. Chairman, I don't think Mr. Staines would know the difference." The crowd roared; Staines had been interrupting and heckling Tommy in a loud voice from the back of the hall.

✍ **Ed Whelan**

Tommy Douglas rides in the Dog Derby at Hudson Bay Junction, Saskatchewan, during the Golden Jubilee celebrations, summer 1955.

SASKATCHEWAN FARMER

Tommy frequently addressed meetings at what was then known as Foster's Grove near Oungre, in the heart of the south country, near the American border, part of Tommy's old provincial Weyburn constituency.

In one speech in the late 1950s, Tommy was addressing the question of what Liberal and Conservative governments in Ottawa had done for Saskatchewan farmers. What could a Saskatchewan farmer expect from the federal government? Tommy put it this way.

"If you take a Saskatchewan farmer and cut him in two and look at him as a piece of bacon, what you would find is three very lean layers and one fat layer—the three lean layers for the years between elections and the fat layer for election year."

That is how Tommy explained it to the people at the meeting. They all understood exactly what he meant.

⚙ **Leroy Durst**

Burns Night

Many people in the Lloydminster area will agree that one of Tommy's outstanding performances was at a Bobbie Burns Day celebration in that city on January 25, 1959.

Station CJNB North Battleford recorded it and played the tape on the air on Burns Day for some years afterwards. I understand that the record eventually wore out.

As Tommy said, "The memory of Bobbie Burns will live forever in the hearts of the Scottish people."

Our hope is that the memory of Tommy Douglas, this beloved Canadian statesman, and his great contribution to the health and well-being of his fellow men, will never be forgotten.

✍ **Chris and Jeanne Delahoy**

Which Hospital?

At a meeting in the Saskatoon Arena, a guy interrupted Douglas numerous times by shouting, "You can't get in the hospital."

Douglas paid no attention for four or five minutes. However, the next time the guy shouted, "You can't get in the hospital," Douglas whirled and said, "You want the wrong hospital—a jackass should obviously go to a veterinary hospital."

✍ **W.A. (Wes) Robbins**

Talking to the Church

We had a presbytery meeting in the Arcola-Estevan Presbytery of the United Church. In those days we used to invite a special speaker in to sort of give us some lift. Tommy had just been elected Premier. Fillmore was quite a Liberal stronghold; when I suggested that we ask him to speak, well, there was a little bit of bristling. They didn't want to hear a political speech but they gave in and invited Tommy, and Tommy addressed the presbytery meeting and we had a good crowd out. I didn't hear a person who didn't have something good to say. Everyone went away just inspired, even the hardest old Liberal who was there.

✍ **Rev. Armand D. Stade**

A Story that Travels

In one of Tommy's election campaigns, I think it was somewhere in Saskatchewan, he was supposed to debate with the Liberal candidate, a hulk of a man. Anyway, in order to try to save face, he looked down at Tommy and said, "Why, you little pip-squeak, I could gobble you up in two big bites." And Tommy's answer to him was, "If you do, you will have more brains in your belly than you have in your head."

Once again Tommy got the biggest applause from the crowd.

✍ **Clarence B. Williams**

Tommy Douglas at the opening of the University of Saskatchewan Hospital in Saskatoon, May 14, 1955.

THINKING CLASS FARMERS

Douglas put it right up to you. He was a tremendous man for doing research when he was working on a speech. He taught people there was really no need to suffer like this. There is a way to do it. There is a way to get around it. It didn't mean you had to step on everybody who doesn't follow your line, but it means that you help those who are all going the same way. Don't just think there's only one road. There's all kinds of roads, there's the co-op road, there's the socialist road and there's even a little space for the capitalist road, since we live in a capitalistic society. He taught people that you could be 10 parts here and 40 here and 40 here and still be a follower. The CCF, you see, was not started by the down and outers. It was started by the thinking class farmers.

And those who bitterly opposed him had to work very, very hard to find reason to hate him, and then when they did that they found reason to be ashamed of themselves.

He really turned society upside down. He made converts by letting people find out about themselves.

✤ **John H. Archer**

The 15th National CCF Convention, Mount Royal Hotel, Montreal, 1958. Tommy Douglas. Standing at back: Roger Provost, secretary, 1946-1949, Quebec CCF (PSD: Le Parti social democratique du Quebec), president, Fédération des Travailleurs du Quebec. Seated at back: Gérard Picard, president, Canadian and Catholic Confederation of Labour; Ran Harding, B.C. CCF MLA; Emile Boudreau; Michael Chartrand, Leader, Quebec CCF; unknown. Seated below: unknown beside Thérèse Casgrain (1896-1981), CCF federal vice-president, 1948-1961, Leader, Quebec CCF, 1951-1957; Pauline Dodge (?), unknown.

YOU'RE A DREAMER

My Tommy Douglas story happened at a meeting in a little school house at Sturgis, Saskatchewan.

Tommy told them, "We're going to harness the Churchill River in the north and mine coal at Estevan, run an electrical grid over all of Saskatchewan."

A large, burly man at the back of the hall stood up, and said, "Mr. Douglas, you're a dreamer."

A number of years later Tommy was back at Sturgis to open a new school. The whole country was lit up. A man came up to Tommy and said, "Do you remember me?"

Tommy said, "You look familiar but I don't remember meeting you."

The man said, "It was a meeting you held in that little school house, and there was a man at the back who got up and said you were a dreamer. That was me. I didn't think you could do it."

⊕ **Hugh Alexander**

GENUINE

I have this image in my mind of Tommy warmly embracing people.

So often you see politicians in the stereotypical waving or just that little temporary touching of hands as they go through the crowd.

Tommy left a genuine impression when he grasped a person's hand or embraced a person: there was such a joy and warmth. That's the feeling he left with me.

Ⓥ **Roy Romanow**

TOMMY AT WINDSOR ONTARIO

In late 1944, Tommy addressed a meeting in Windsor, Ontario when I was on the Essex County CCF Council.

Many people from Saskatchewan because of the Depression had gone to work in Windsor when the war started. They all came to hear Tommy. Jimmie from Colgate, Saskatchewan, invited me to the meeting. The hall was full. Tommy entertained us and educated us and, I guess basically, his personality and his approach fascinated and convinced us. After the meeting, people gathered around Tommy, farmers and the sons and daughters of farmers he had known in Saskatchewan. There was much handshaking and a lot to talk about "now that the CCF is the government in Saskatchewan."

✎ **Ed Whelan**

FOLLOWED THROUGH

I think Tommy Douglas understood the farmers. He never pretended at any time that he was a farmer but the farmers trusted him. Why?

On account of his honesty. When he said something he followed through. At that time people had pretty well given up, there was so much pressure on them, but after listening to him, he would give you new hope that there were better things.

Ⓥ **R.A. Cugnet**

RETURNING TO THE CHURCH AS PREMIER

I can remember that he always started a sermon with a little joke. He had his special little type of joke and there were several types, for his church, for his political meetings, and for other times. I think that his messages were lightened up because he had this part at the beginning to get everybody in good humour.

Everything was down to earth. He talked of social justice for everyone, and everyone being on the same level; no one was better than the other one. He gave us a lot of that in his sermons.

Ⓥ **Helen Davidson**

TRUCKERS

When Tommy brought in automobile insurance, my brother and I were at this meeting. All these truckers were there. Tommy was a little late and the language, well, it got scary. I said, "George, we'd better watch it."

They were having the odd beer. I can still see that hall when Tommy comes in the door. He walks to the stage like the bantam fighter he was, and grabs the microphone adjusting it, and looks around at the crowd. He starts to tell one of his little, fairly light jokes to these stone-wall faces staring at him. Then he just jumps right into the meat, you know, what he was going to say.

I never saw a guy who could take a crowd like that! Ten minutes—one guy would forget himself and clap and then he would shrink back and the other guys would look at him.

They got carried away. He was telling them, "We send our insurance money down there to Chicago and Detroit and Toronto and Montreal. Do you like sending your money down there? You know what we can do with the money here."

In that succinct, clear way he just took that crowd and had them cheering and carrying him out of that building.

Do you know anyone else who could have done that?

⚙ **Percy Brown**

BANNOCKBURN RECALLED

When Tommy was Minister of Co-ops we had the Trade and Marketing Division, which encouraged support of the Hudson Bay Route.

A great friend of the Hudson Bay Route

Tommy Douglas in front of the fireplace in the government members' lounge at the Saskatchewan Legislature, 1961.

was R.T. Dalgliesh, well-known ship owner of Newcastle-on-Tyne. He used to come to Saskatchewan every year; we would arrange a schedule of meetings for him. On one occasion, Tommy arranged for a dinner at the Hotel Saskatchewan to enable Dalgliesh to meet importers who would be likely to order goods from England to be carried by Dalgliesh ships.

Tommy said he welcomed the appearance of Dalgliesh. It served as a reminder of the feat of Roger Bannister, an Englishman. (This was a short time after Roger Bannister ran the four-minute mile.) Bannister, he said, had run faster than any Englishman had run since the Battle of Bannockburn! Dalgliesh almost fell out of his chair.

⚙ **B.N. (Barney) Arnason**

Tommy and the CCF Party

TOMMY AND CLARENCE FINES

Each one had a role to play, an unwritten contract, there was one area which was Tommy's, the political leadership; there was one area that was Clarence's, that was party organization. There was tremendous respect. Tommy had no desire to be a manager, and he wasn't. And Clarence had no ambition to be party leader.

So you had this complete confidence between the two and, if an issue came up in one area where the other guy was asked the question, you were immediately referred. Clarence would say, "Take that up with the Premier." And Tommy would say, if it was a matter of public expenditures or anything of that sort, "We'll talk it over with Clarence."

I asked Tommy if they had ever sat down and agreed on how they would operate. He said, "No, we worked together. We each knew what we could do and that is all we needed."

⚭ **T.H. (Tommy) McLeod**

TOMMY AND PROVINCIAL COUNCIL

About 1948, I was elected to Provincial Council. Tommy as Premier and Leader of the Party attended every meeting. Each of us had an opportunity to meet him because he sat and talked to individual councillors. He made people feel at home.

Each year before the House opened, the legislative program and budget were dealt with by Council. Tommy had every piece of legislation introduced by the minister responsible. The skeleton budget was brought to Council. Council went over both carefully and if they turned something down, it didn't go any further.

Tommy used Council as a sounding board and used it effectively. He listened. He never took part in a debate until he felt it was absolutely necessary. And, of course, he gained nothing but respect from the people who were there. They were there to represent their constituencies and the Party, and Tommy acknowledged this completely. When he thought they were off base, he would give his point of view, saying, "You may be right but this is the position as I see it."

✏ **Ed Whelan**

Tommy, Shirley and Irma at home in Weyburn after the 1944 election.

THE DOUGLAS HOUSE

I got to know Tommy and Irma, Joan and Shirley a bit, while I was in Saskatchewan in the mid-1950s. While travelling the countryside for the CCF, I would return often to Regina late Friday or early Saturday, eager to brief Tommy on the latest. I would hesitate to phone too early in the morning. Once, when I phoned at 8:30 am I asked Irma if Tommy was still sleeping. She said he was, and then said, "Oh, here he comes." Tommy, having just awakened, bubbled over with enthusiasm and asked me about a number of people in the communities I had just visited.

I travelled to many a meeting with him in his car and delighted in his conversation, sometimes light, sometimes very serious. Working with him was an experience of a lifetime. One recognized his awareness of the people he served and his closeness with his own family.

✎ **Magnus Eliason**

HE OPENED HIS WALLET

My first experience with Tommy was that first year I was a candidate in the provincial campaign in 1956. They scheduled Tommy to speak in Leader. I got a message from Tim Lee a few days before. Would I please be in Leader by about 4:00 o'clock that afternoon. Mr. Douglas would like to see me.

Dr. Hugh MacLean, Tommy Douglas, Frank R. Scott, Clarence Fines, John W. Corman, John Sturdy, Shirley and Irma Douglas after swearing in of the new CCF government in Saskatchewan, July 10, 1944.

"Oh no!" I thought maybe I had done something wrong. I went to the hotel and I asked for Tim Lee. Tim took me into Tommy's room and we sat. Tommy asked me a whole slew of questions. How was the campaign going? How was I making out personally?

I replied, "Not so hot personally," as we were broke, both me and the constituency organization. Then we went on talking of other things.

Just before I left, Tommy reached in his pocket, opened his wallet and gave me $200. Under other circumstances I wouldn't have taken it. But I had been charging up gas bills for the car and we were a month behind in the rent and I wasn't going to ask relatives for money. I don't know how many leaders would have been that thoughtful and showed that much direct interest in someone else's personal affairs.

Many years later we had a 'do' for Tommy and Irma. I said, "This is the measure of this man," and recited this story. When

Tommy got up, he turned, looked at me and said, "You know I had forgotten all about that. You never did give me back that $200." He kept a poker face.

✍ **Les Benjamin**

PREMIER AND PRESIDENT

Influence outside Caucus came from people like Carlyle King, president of the Party. He always had an invitation and was welcomed when there was some issue he felt strongly about. Tommy always treated Carlyle with respect.

As the elected leader of the Party, Tommy was the political leader, and he and the president had to work together and understand one another. And they did. Tommy respected Carlyle and Carlyle respected Tommy and they worked together very well.

(Over the years they met regularly, on Saturday afternoon in Tommy's office.)

✍ **Ed Whelan**

Helping Hand

In 1952, I took on the position of Secretary-Treasurer for the Shellbrook Constituency CCF and held it for 27 years. I remember Tommy coming to speak at one of our conventions. I was green at the secretarial job and was trying to get my minutes and resolutions in order before leaving the hall. Tommy came over and said, "Can I give you a hand, lad?" His driver was waiting for him, but he took time to help me work things out.

I was at the rally in Regina in 1983 when we said farewell to Tommy. Though he was ill, he gave a tremendous address. I shook his hand and he said, "You're from Shellbrook, aren't you?" What a wonderful memory! What a wonderful man!

✍ **Bert Mason**

Legislative Advisory Committee

The Legislative Advisory Committee was set up in 1944 at the convention after the election. There were three of us,- Mrs. Gertrude Telford, Charlie Broughton and I was chairman.

Tommy consulted us about changes in the Cabinet or the appointment of a deputy minister, or when a new piece of legislation was giving him trouble. We met three or four times a year in Tommy's office, for an hour and a half.

☸ **Cliff Thurston**

The Douglas Club

We met Tommy Douglas away back in the 1930s at Kayville before he was an MP. Somewhere in there, I (Tom) took J.S. Woodsworth and Clarence Fines around the country. I drove them in a buggy. In those days I knew quite a few politicians around the district. But there was no comparison with Tommy's speaking. And when he said something you knew that he intended to do it, that was what he was going to do if at all possible.

After we moved to Regina, Premier Douglas used to come to the Douglas Club to church banquets. If he was in town we always asked him.

The Douglas Club was organized from the Romanian Club and we had people from the other clubs, the Hungarian, the Victoria Club, the Ukrainian Club. I don't know how we came to call it the "Douglas Club."

When Tommy Douglas came to speak, the place was always full.

☸ **Tom and Mary Banda**

Campaign Yardsticks

Tommy had a couple of election campaign yardsticks. He told candidates, "The others are volunteers, you've got to work harder than they do, you've got to lead them."

He sometimes said, "It's all right to be angry in the campaign because you have only 34 days to win or lose. Everything is riding on that. You have only so many days, it's like putting your title on the line for all the volunteers and those who put up their dollars and their time."

✍ **Ed Whelan**

2:00 AM CALL

Tommy was a tough guy to work for. In one campaign I thought I was doing a good job as Provincial Secretary. Then Tommy would go to a meeting. He'd come back home and phone at two or three o'clock in the morning and there is nothing worse than a two or three o'clock call in the morning and falling out of bed. When it's the Premier of the Province, it just shakes you right to the core.

The second time it happened I thought, well that's enough of this. I got all the stuff together, dashed up to his office. He was sitting behind his desk. Eleanor McKinnon was outside, and she looked at me and said, "Somebody's in there. He will be right out."

I wanted to go in there while I was good and mad because I was going to throw it down on his desk and tell him that this has to be the last time I worked like this.

Tommy looked up at me, and he looked again. He straightened up and said, "You're mad. I've never seen you mad before."

He came around his desk and he said, "Have you had your breakfast yet?"

I said, "No."

"I haven't either," he said, "let's go down and have breakfast."

He threw his papers down on the desk, put his arm around my shoulder, and down we went. We never mentioned anything about the phone call.

⚖ **Percy Brown**

THE WAR YEARS

During the long lonely winter months of the war years Dad and I listened to the radio, following the rising dynamic young politician, Tommy Douglas, and went to local political meetings.

It was J.H. Brockelbank who, at one meeting, urged me to attend a CCF school to be held in Moose Jaw and soon I became involved in organizational work.

I tried to explain, in my letters Overseas, the high hopes for the future that the CCF held out for us, of our dreams and ideals for a better world, the world that my husband was fighting to keep free. I urged him to be sure and vote in the Overseas elections and wrote endlessly of the wonderful new leader, Tommy Douglas.

I found it very difficult in those years to decide just where my duty lay: home with the children, on the land with my dad, political organization, teaching school, as teachers were terribly scarce. Oh dear! What? What? What?

One day I had the opportunity to talk over my problems with Tommy. His sympathy and understanding were as valuable as his good counsel.

Among other things I remember he said, "There is no one way to service, Olive, there are many ways, and as long as you recognize that you have a duty to serve your fellow men you can be trusted to choose the 'right' way."

✍ **Olive E. Wells**

CCF HEADQUARTERS

In the 1930s our home in the Wynyard district was the CCF headquarters, nobody even thought of using the hotel in those days. George Williams, M.J. Coldwell, Tommy Douglas and many other CCFers stayed with us.

Barney and I never missed a Douglas meeting, unless it was impossible to go. Tommy was a man with a mission, who didn't let anything get in the way. He was full of wisdom and he never let anyone down.

Medicare was Tommy's greatest contribution. He didn't care where the credit went; he wanted to accomplish something, and he did make the world better.

⊕ **Beth (Mrs. Barney) Johnson**

PLATFORM CARD

The 1952 election, as I recall it, was the first one where Tommy brought out the little white card saying, "Here's what we are going to do with these particular targets, what we are going to accomplish." And they were not pie-in-the-sky targets because there had been a good deal of analysis going into what was feasible.

I remember in the 1956 election he said, "This is what we promised we would do in 1952 and this is what we did. We exceeded that target; we were a little short there. Here's our planned platform for the next four years."

It was a good approach. Tommy had credibility because he had been able to deliver.

⊕ **T.K. Shoyama**

TOMMY ON PATRONAGE

I recall Tommy's vehement position on patronage. In the early days of the CCF administration there was a conflict within the Regina CCF as to whether the government was looking after "our people." Some of the executive wanted the old system and the executive was split. But Tommy was adamant. He wasn't going to change and neither was Clarence Fines. M.J. Coldwell had been a member of the commission that brought about the formation of the Public Service Commission, but it had not been operating the way it should have until Mr. Douglas came along and said: this is an important part of CCF policy.

I can recall when some members of the Provincial Executive were unhappy about the appointment of a person they thought was not politically attuned. Tommy very bluntly told them, that as far as he was concerned, the man had the qualifications and he was going to get the job.

⊕ **George R. Bothwell**

DOUGLAS RALLY

In the 1956 election we held our Douglas Rally in Kelliher, just a day or so before the election. The old hall was packed. In the question period a questioner tried to beat Tommy up with the Communist party. The questioner tried to stop Tommy from answering. Tommy with his famous little giggle told him "to let one fool at a time talk." The questioner immediately accused Tommy of calling him a fool. The crowd went into hysterics and one heckler left the hall, his head hanging.

✍ **Frank Meakes**

A Special Tray

During the 1975 provincial election campaign Tommy came to speak in North Battleford. The Douglas-Kramer Young New Democrats presented Tommy with two items, the first was an "I'm for Kramer" t-shirt, the second was a silver serving tray.

After some debate at the club meeting, I was chosen to present Tommy with the tray. For days I walked on clouds.

The tray had been ordered from a local jewellery store and we had jointly written the inscription to be put on it: "To Tommy Douglas, in appreciation for your many long years of service to and for the youth of Saskatchewan. The Douglas-Kramer Young New Democrats." On the afternoon of the rally I picked up the tray. Imagine my concern when I discovered the last line,-"The Douglas-Kramer Young New Democrates." To get a new tray engraved before the evening was impossible. We decided to present the tray to Tommy and then ask for it back—get a new tray done and send it on to him.

I had the rather dubious honour of asking for the tray back (as well as presenting it).

Following the meeting I explained the spelling error to Tommy and said we would like to take it back.

Tommy smiled and said, "No, you can't have it back. I noticed the error. I have received quite a few serving trays, but I've never received one with a spelling error. I want to keep it, it's special."

Those of us in the club at the time still relate this story to one another. It reminds us that a gracious, caring person can make a bunch of young people feel really special, even when they do make a mistake.

✍ **Merril Dean**

Tommy Douglas visiting the Fort Black Co-op Store in Ile-a-la-Crosse, Saskatchewan. This Co-op broke the monopoly of the Hudson's Bay Co. in the community.

Tommy and the MLAs

THE ENDS OF THE EARTH

In 1946 following my discharge from the Armed Services, I had the opportunity to watch the proceedings of the Legislature from the public gallery on many occasions; I developed an admiration for Tommy Douglas which approached hero worship.

His mere presence in the House provided an aura of dignity and respect, and the jabs and thrusts of debate displayed Tommy as the undisputed master of the House.

It was 14 years later that I became a candidate for the CCF in 1960. The election was fought and won on Tommy's promise to introduce the first pre-paid Medical Care Plan in North America. I recall with clarity my maiden speech in the Legislature. With considerable trepidation and sweaty palms, I rose in my place to deliver a 25 minute speech which had been three weeks in preparation.

In retrospect, I would say now that it was not an extraordinary effort, but afterward, Tommy, in his warm, generous and genuine manner, offered a handclasp and words of encouragement and congratulation.

This for me represents one of the early and lasting memories I have of Tommy, a gesture which lifted the spirits of a young and green politician, and convinced him that he would follow Tommy to the ends of the earth.

✍ **Gordon T. Snyder**

CROSSING THE FLOOR

At the time Ross Thatcher had decided to cross the floor in the House of Commons, M.J. Coldwell came to the house one day. He talked to father, C.M. Fines, for a while and he told him a story that I listened to with some interest, as I had never heard the term "cross the floor" before.

When they were finished, they called Tommy over. M.J. Coldwell repeated the same story, that Ross Thatcher was causing all kinds of problems at Ottawa, and was going to cross the floor. But he had indicated that if he were allowed to run provincially in Moose Jaw, if he were elected and if we would guarantee him a cabinet position, he would not cross the floor.

Tommy gave the final word: "No, we don't want him, no matter what kind of problems he is going to cause. He's not a person we want in our cabinet."

Coldwell said, "Well, he'll cross the floor."

"That's fine."

In my opinion, this is the reason that Ross Thatcher had such a vendetta against the CCF government of Saskatchewan.

☿ **Murray Fines**

Marjorie Cooper, Regina MLA, 1952 to 1967.

ENCOURAGING MLAs

Tommy was very attentive when members were speaking and very encouraging if he thought you had put a lot of work on your speech and had made some good points.

The page would come along with a little note—"I particularly liked this"—or —"You did a good job." He was very good at that. He was extremely thoughtful.

He would turn his chair and sit and watch you as you spoke. Most premiers would never have time to do it, but he made the time. I think he got more work from his members because he showed an interest in them and what they were doing.

        ✺ **Marjorie Cooper Hunt**

FIRST MINISTER

What was he like as the first minister around the cabinet table?

He mediated—but he also led. He's had even greater skill in making clear the ramifications of complex matters. Sometimes he asked much of his ministers, but few, if any of us ever thought he asked too much.

        ✂ **Woodrow S. Lloyd**

STAND UP, SPEAK UP

When I first came to the Saskatchewan Legislature in 1960 Tommy Douglas was Premier. He established a relationship with his members, particularly with the new members. There were a couple of little things he'd tell all the new members and the entire Caucus. "If you are making a speech, you should stand up, speak up and shut up."

He would say that a speech should follow a general outline as Sir Wilfrid Laurier had said: "Tell them what you are going to tell them; tell them; and then tell them what you told them."

That's what Tommy did. He would say, "I am going to outline three points and these are my three points. And then I am going to expand on these three points so you will understand what they are and what it is all about." At the end he would summarize. As a result, you remembered the three points he had made.

        ✺ **Ed Whelan**

I CHOSE SASKATCHEWAN

I heard about Tommy from my father who had been a strong supporter of Douglas. Dad was a strong trade unionist in Toronto, and had been one of the pushers to get Douglas as the leader of the national party when the NDP came into being.

I came to Saskatchewan in 1965, the year I was ordained. Our church had a system of transferring people to where they were needed. Make your choice known, they suggested. I happened to choose Saskatchewan. So that is how I came to be in Eatonia.

Had been at Eatonia a couple of years, I guess, when I started to take part in activities in the NDP constituency.

In 1971, when I was running (it was then Kindersley constituency, before it became Kindersley-Kerrobert), the only politician of any stature who would take time to come to speak was Tommy Douglas.

Now, that was in a day when Tommy was tiring a little more readily, but he came. He didn't come in, as some politicians do, just at the time of the speech, expecting to go to the stage and speak and leave. He came early, he visited the people who were there, he went around the hall, and he did the same thing at the end of the meeting.

And that was certainly a lesson to me on how to be a politician, on how to relate to people. You could see that people responded to Tommy and we had people out who were not New Democrats, but they responded to Tommy Douglas.

🜨 **Alex Taylor**

CURE FOR INSOMNIA

The Leader of the Opposition was going on and on. Tommy was sitting back with his eyes closed. We had radio at that time. The Leader of the Opposition said, "The Premier is asleep in his seat." Tommy opened his eyes and jumped to his feet. "Privilege, Mr. Speaker. I'm not asleep, but I wish I were. The speeches of the Hon. Member ought to be recorded and he ought to sell them. They're the greatest cure for insomnia that I can think of."

🜨 **Eiling Kramer**

ELECTED MEMBER COMES FIRST

I will never forget the first time I went to see Tommy in his office after I was elected in 1960. Eleanor McKinnon said, "Ed Whelan, the MLA for Regina, is here." I heard Tommy on the intercom say, "Well, all I have in here are a couple of civil servants and I will ask them to leave." He sent them away and ushered me in with one hand out and the other hand on my shoulder. He said, "What's your problem?" All the time Tommy was Premier, I could get to see him if he was there, no matter who was in his office.

This convinced me that an elected member came first.

✍ **Ed Whelan**

Clarence Fines and Tommy in 1960.

CAUCUS WAS DEMOCRATIC

In Caucus, Tommy was never the chairman. He was present most of the time and was very democratic. He was a very good listener. If he felt strongly on something he usually got his way, simply because he was so persuasive he made you feel his way was right. If he felt you had a good point, he was willing to compromise. He couldn't be pushed around, I can tell you, but he was willing to compromise.

✍ **Marjorie Cooper Hunt**

TOMMY IN CAUCUS

Tommy let his ministers handle their own legislation and their own resolutions. The Caucus members admired Tommy, he was on a personal basis with each member.

Tommy was looked upon in Caucus as leader but also he said little things that sort of endeared him to members. For instance, if Marjorie Cooper came in late,- Marjorie Cooper was very pro-temperance and never drank,- he would say, "I see Marjorie is late again, she's been in the bar." It was funny coming from Tommy Douglas because he never drank.

He had ways of kidding members and contradicting them in the kindest, gentlest way. He knew how to differ with individual members of Caucus without showing them up, without humiliating them. They liked him for it. That didn't stop him from disagreeing with them but he was always considerate.

✍ **Ed Whelan**

DECISIONS IN CAUCUS

Most of the time there wasn't too sharp an area of difference and there wouldn't be a division. But if there was a division and it was on an important issue and there were say 18 votes for and 16 against, Tommy wouldn't proceed. He would have to have a much stronger decision than that. He would say, "Well, obviously there is considerable opposition and we will just put that on the table." Then he would say, "If you will agree, we will consult the chairman and put it on the agenda. We will have another look at it." He'd say, "We haven't done this right," or, "It isn't acceptable to enough of the Caucus." He did this—I can remember a number of instances—and he did it well.

✍ **Ed Whelan**

PLANNING A SPEECH

He planned everything. I once asked Tommy how much of all this is something that is extemporaneous? And he said, "Well, when I go out for a main speech in the spring or the fall, I will work on that on Saturday or Sunday with Eleanor. She will type it and I'll make some changes and she'll type it again. Then I'll go over it and I'll make some notes."

And Tommy had a good memory, you see. To hear him it looked as though all this was coming out ad lib, you know, without any particular study. But not so. He did a great deal of preparation.

⚪ **W.G. (Bill) Davies**

Tommy visits the International Mineral and Chemical Corporation (IMCC) mine near Esterhazy, 1961.

LEARNING FROM TOMMY

I learned two or three things from Douglas. First, he certainly impressed me when he said—and he is not the only person who has said this—that faith has to be something you do, not something you talk about. That struck a chord with me.

One of the other things and I got this secondhand from a person who used to be an executive member of the Saskatchewan Government Employees' Association, who said the only time that Douglas had ever ripped him out was when he dared to question Tommy's motives. Then, he said, Douglas went up one side of him and down the other.

I remember, on another occasion, Tommy talking about taking people at face value, accepting what they say, though not liking it; fighting what they say but not attacking the individual's motives. That taught me a lesson which I think is important for most of us in life and certainly for politicians. It is not to try to read into other people's motives, but simply to go on with what you think is right, and give them the right to have their position. Douglas, you know, could be a fantastic campaigner and fighter but he never tried to suggest that the other person did not have a right to differ.

When Tommy gave an uppercut, it was an uppercut to the argument, to the truthfulness or lack of it. It was never an uppercut to the person and, to me, that is one of the things I always respected very much about Tommy. That and, the third thing, would be just the way he cared for ordinary people, in the way he would put himself out for them.

⚪ **Alex Taylor**

LIVING THE EXAMPLE

The main thing about Tommy, I think, was that he always saw himself as one who needed to provide a constant example. He had to be a person who not only put his money where his mouth was, but who lived the kind of a life that he thought and suggested should be led by everyone.

He was very, very sensitive to any kind of thing that would detract from that image. I think Tommy, in a very good sense, was a considerable actor and saw himself as a player. I suppose this isn't unusual. But I am positive that Tommy, quite often, much more than many other people, weighed every action. And you could see it in government.

One of the things watched when we first took power, gifts to civil servants and politicians, was virtually cut out. Anything that was a gift, any largesse around Christmas time, could not have a value of more than $10.00.

W.G. (Bill) Davies

A VERY SPECIAL PERSON

He was probably the finest debater that the House has seen. A fine voice, a great flow of language, a copious knowledge of the King James version of the Bible and of the Protestant hymns, a substantial knowledge of poetry —of Burns, but of many others—allowed him to sparkle his oratory with apt quotations.

. . . In government, as a premier, as an administrator, he was razor-sharp, being able to dissect a balance sheet within a minute or two. And I've seen him do it, and I've seen him question me on it and go to the heart of the balance sheet almost immediately. He demanded and got top-level performance from the people who worked around him. He was quite capable of being demanding and hard-driving—sometimes unreasonably so, perhaps, seen from the other side of the fence because he certainly demanded performance. But he commanded a respect by all, and an affection by most, that made him a pleasure to work with, and a very special person.

. . . I'm proud to have known this pugnacious premier who fought the good fight with all his might for the things in which he believed.

Allan E. Blakeney

LEGISLATIVE LIBRARIAN

Everyone was saying nice things about John Archer. He was leaving the Legislative Library to go to Queen's University. He was well liked and had been helpful to all Members of the Legislature. As Tommy would say, they were pouring a gallon of syrup on a lone pancake.

They were overdoing it; one backbencher on our side of the House said, "John Archer has been most helpful to me," and went on and on. At the conclusion this member said, "Yes, I find if you want information you go to the Library, if you want the right information you go to the horse's mouth."

Quick as a flash Tommy said, "I'm glad you got the right end of the horse!"

There was no more syrup!

Ed Whelan

A CCF Government:
Civil Service and Administration

THE CCF AND LEADER

The thing that always amazed me, while I was there, was a tremendous spirit of progressiveness that seemed to be present across the whole of the government. I suppose this stemmed from Mr. Douglas, it stemmed to some extent from the CCF movement itself, a movement which deliberately went out to make things better for everybody. You saw an extraordinary group of civil servants, in addition to some pretty extraordinary politicians. A lot of things that happened in the rest of Canada just followed on as a result of what happened in Saskatchewan. A lot of that was the CCF movement, but an awful lot of it was T.C. Douglas.

⊛ **Dr. Burns Roth**

OVERLY DEMOCRATIC

Tommy Douglas was the essence of a democrat, he really was. Of all the years that I was cabinet secretary, I really never saw him take advantage of his position. I never saw him become authoritarian. Probably, if he had been a little more authoritarian than he was, he might have speeded things up a little. It was his choice to be overly democratic.

⊛ **H.S. (Tim) Lee**

TOMMY'S STRENGTH

One thing I think shows Tommy's strength. Before 1944 he appointed party committees, different committees for different things. Joe Phelps, for instance, on Natural Resources and Industrial Development. Joe's committee worked. They were ready to recommend all kinds of things so that when the government came into power, the work had already been done. I had been given the task of heading up the Committee on Finance and Taxation. I had half a dozen recommendations ready for Cabinet. This was where Tommy really shone and the success we had in our earliest days was because we had done the work ahead of time.

Tommy was always great at getting a consensus of opinion among people that might have many different ideas to start. We would be going to a meeting of Cabinet with 12 members, and probably four or five different ideas. Tommy had the happy facility of being able to take those four ideas and say, "Now A, you wanted to get this, but you don't want that. Would you like to go a little further this way? B, you wanted part of what A wanted here, but you'd go a little faster on this and not quite so fast here." When he had finished, he had them all wanting the same thing. I admired him greatly for his ability to get a consensus.

⊛ **C.M. Fines**

An Economist Listens

I got my army discharge in August 1946 and that's when I began my career with the Saskatchewan government. Tommy McLeod offered me a job as an Economic Research Assistant at $150.00 a month.

I remember when I first heard Tommy Douglas speak, in early September of 1946. I was living on Montague Street, Regina, not far from Scott Collegiate. Tommy was to speak in Scott Collegiate. I was staying with George Tamaki at the time. George said, "Why don't we go along and listen." I said, "Sure, that would be very interesting." I remember that meeting very vividly. It was a packed auditorium.

I remember when he quoted from William Blake, you know, "journeying through Jerusalem, his sword would not lie in his sheath," and I must admit, I was really transfixed. Of course, as you know, he could always sort of warm up the audience with engaging stories and everybody was in a cheerful mood, then he went on, got into the serious part of what the CCF government was trying to do, the difficulty it was facing, the need for the people to support it.

I said to myself, "Here's the man that I'm going to work for and follow." Absolutely. When I heard his speech and, you know, what he said always made a great deal of sense,- there was logic, coherence, clarity in the way he spoke. It wasn't a rambling diatribe one hears so often these days. There was a structure to his speech, ideas that were logically developed and coherently expressed and, of course, the emotion that he could evoke. I was convinced that not only was I lucky, I was privileged to be working in his government.

⚘ **T.K. Shoyama**

Fair Pay

Charwomen (as they were then called) had been told not to come to work at the Legislative Building during winter blizzards but had been docked pay. One of them had written T.C. Douglas complaining about the unfairness.

Tommy sent a memo to the Minister of Public Works on March 14, 1947: "Would you kindly let me have an explanation."

The Minister replied on March 14, 1947: "Arrangements have been made to compensate these women."

SAB **Douglas Papers**

Bureaucrat's Viewpoint

My principal contact with the Premier was through sitting on the Treasury Board. Of course he was fascinating, everybody knows that, and all of us absolutely worshipped him. From a bureaucrat's point of view, he wasn't an easy person to work for. If there was a complaint from the public, his first assumption was that the bureaucrat was wrong. The burden of proof was on you. Now, when he had the facts and you were able to make a case, he was quite willing to support you. And having worked with a good many ministers since, I have come to appreciate how sound that posture is for a politician.

At times many of us became quite irritated. That would dissipate very quickly when he would come down to the cafeteria and sit down with four or five of us at a table and talk about important things and humourous things. Whatever ill feeling we might have had would soon be gone.

⚘ **Don Tansley**

came out of the Executive Council Chambers.

I said, "Go back in. There's a man here with a gun."

Nothing frightened Tommy; he went out the door trying to catch up with the man.

⊛ **Eleanor McKinnon**

Eleanor McKinnon, secretary to the Premier, and Tommy in the office.

MAN WITH A GUN

One day Zina McMurtry (secretary to J.T. Douglas, Minister of Highways) phoned me and said, "There's a man on his way to your office. He has a gun and a handful of cartridges and he said, 'I'm going to shoot the bastard (referring to the Premier)'."

I called through on the intercom to Tim Lee and said, "Perhaps you'd better phone the police."

The man came flying into our office. He was excited and angry. I treated him as calmly as I could and told him that the Premier was tied up in a cabinet meeting (which he was), and prayed he wouldn't come out.

I persuaded the man to see Dr. McKerracher who was Director of Psychiatric Services. He was able to get the man out of the office. The door had just closed when Tommy

VERY HUMAN

I thought Mr. Douglas was a human person, very human. Of course, he was also humanitarian. He could talk to anybody and talk their language and their topics. He could talk to an egg head. And then he could talk to an ordinary person and they all understood him and they all liked him.

He had that Christian approach, he was kind. He didn't like people being abused in any shape or form. He believed in fair play and certainly he believed in social justice. He did say that a lot of social injustices stemmed from the fact that there was economic injustice.

I do believe that Tommy and the CCF recruited the finest crew of civil servants in the history of Saskatchewan.

⊛ **T.S. (Tom) Tamaki**

PLANNING CONFERENCE

The Saskatchewan CCF government had determined that it needed to address the problems of planning in a coherent, structured way and, for that purpose every fall it would hold a week-long planning session in which the departments would be asked to present their policy proposals and projections and program ideas.

The office I was working with, the Economic Advisory and Planning Board, had the responsibility of trying to co-ordinate this and to provide, of course, the broader overview of the economy, where we thought the Saskatchewan economy was likely to go in the immediate year ahead, and then try some longer term projections, four or five years down the road.

We had what was called the Annual Cabinet Planning Board Conference in November of every year. This is where I saw Tommy at his, shall I say, professional best, because he chaired these things as the leader.

It was interesting to see how quickly he would grasp the technical ideas, how quickly he could focus on the real policy issues. He would ask questions that in a sense almost embarrassed the professionals because he was asking questions about things that they had not really thought about. It was always just a marvellous experience and you learned a great deal about policy planning, how to focus on ideas, how to develop ideas.

✇ **T.K. Shoyama**

AFRAID?

Every year they had the Cabinet Planning Board Conference.

They were all busy and of course they had phone calls coming. If we called them out, it disrupted the conference. So Tommy told me not to call anyone out, unless it was a matter of life or death.

Mr. Joe Phelps (Minister of Natural Resources) swung in, tossed his hat on the hat tree, and said, "I'm expecting an urgent call. Call me out the moment it comes in."

The call came through and I went to Mr. Phelps and whispered that his call had come through.

Tommy beckoned to me, so I went over.

"I thought I told you not to call anyone out unless it was a matter of life or death."

I said, "I know, but Mr. Phelps told me to call him out when his call came through and I'm much more afraid of him than I am of you," and out I went.

✇ **Eleanor McKinnon**

COMMUNICATION

I had just been hired to work with the Department of Co-operation, based in Buffalo Narrows, having recently left the Hudson's Bay Company.

I was invited to Regina to attend the Department's Christmas party. I was still in the very early stages of probation. I could not really believe I would meet the Premier until it actually happened. He didn't just shake my hand and say he was glad to meet me, he made me believe it was true. He told me to call him "Tommy," and that, if I did not drink, it might be best to avoid the fruit punch, "they" were always trying to make him try it, so there must be something going on.

I think I would have worked for him for nothing. After the years of 'mister-*ing*' and 'sir-*ing*' with the HBC, this was a wonderful revelation for me. The people around me now actually had real concern for northern native people and obviously did not accept the derogatory label applied by most people.

Mr. Douglas (Tommy was always difficult for me to use) promised to attend the next annual meeting of Co-op stores in my district, Ile-a-la-Crosse, Buffalo Narrows and La Loche. At the time, I thought he was just being polite and did not really intend to follow up.

The first meeting was at Ile-a-la-Crosse. The mission hall was crowded to the walls. I think all the people of the community were there. This was my first annual meeting, and to say I was nervous was a major understatement. We quickly got through the business part of the meeting.

Tommy addressed the meeting and either had people so quiet you could hear a pin drop, or else had everyone laughing. It was really wonderful. I learned more that day about communication than I have in the 30 years since.

Tommy repeated the performance at Buffalo Narrows and La Loche. I am sure most people of the area remember the visit as vividly as I do.

✍ **Gerry Parsons**

FIRST EXECUTIVE ASSISTANT

Douglas established an open-door policy. If you want to talk to the Government of Saskatchewan, come and talk to them. And the people took him seriously.

When I accepted the offer to be his Executive Assistant, I said, "What would you like me to do?"

He said, "You know, I really don't know, but I'm getting swamped because all these years I have said to people if you want to talk to me, come and see me. If you have a problem, come and see me. If there is something that is really bothering you, I would like to know about it. People are beginning to accept that invitation. That's what I want you to help me solve."

He said, "Watch out for the farmer who will drive 400 miles to come to Regina with a problem that he could have solved by dropping me a postcard. The problem, to him, is important. It may not be to you, but it is to him. You have to treat that very seriously."

☮ **H.S. (Tim) Lee**

DISASTER INTO SUCCESS

In 1946, I had just joined the Department of Co-operation in Regina. For orientation, they sent me to Saskatoon to attend the Canadian Co-operative Conference. Delegates and visitors came from all across Canada, the United States and Europe. The conference ended with a banquet in the Bessborough Hotel at which Mr. Douglas was the guest speaker.

After dinner, before Mr. Douglas spoke, the organizers of the conference presented an oil painting to one of the long-time co-operators. He rose to thank them for their gift. He spoke at length of his many years of work, and thanked them. He spoke of the work his wife had done, and chastised them for neglecting her. He droned on for nearly an hour until the audience was near rebellion.

Then it was the Premier's turn. He got up and told jokes for ten minutes until everyone was aching with laughter. Then he said that he thought it had been a good conference, and he was sure people were ready to leave. He would speak no more.

Before he rose to speak, the audience had been angry, bored and uncomfortable from sitting. Now they had loosened up and wanted to hear him. They clapped and called for a speech. He consented, but asked people to first stand and move around. Then he shortened his after dinner speech to no more than 15 minutes. There was thunderous applause. He had changed disaster into overwhelming success.

✍ **Jean Larmour**

JUST ONE OF THE GANG

You, sir, more than any other individual, are responsible for the right of government employees in Saskatchewan to bargain collectively—a right, I may say, the employees of no other constitutional government in Canada as yet enjoy. It was given to you in 1944, in a great flash of insight, to perceive that government employees could be entrusted with the right to bargain collectively in the same manner as non-government employees.

It has not been an uncommon sight during the past 17 years for visitors to the Dome Cafe to see you having lunch surrounded by the employees and laughing and chatting with them . . . a casual visitor, unless he knew you, would never realize that here was the Premier of Saskatchewan—just one of the gang.

Your door has always been open to us. When we have been troubled and unsure of ourselves we knew that we could always see you personally.

These few words, sir, do not do justice to the warmth of our regard and affection for you. . . I have the honour of presenting to you an illuminated address, and a gift in the form of two Canada Savings Bonds ($2,000). . . The money for the bonds has been derived from voluntary subscriptions.

✂ **William Leonard**

IN THE CAFETERIA

It used to be that the members of the Cabinet ate in the Cabinet dining room next to the cafeteria, but Tommy broke with tradition. He came out and ate with the common folks.

⚘ **George R. Bothwell**

FIRESIDE CHATS

I had to stand up to open the mail in the mornings. You wouldn't believe the amount of mail we got . . . then he got into the fireside chats which were very, very interesting. They were so popular that everybody wrote in; they'd like this poem or that poem.

Everything he did inspired a great deal of correspondence.

⓪ **Eleanor McKinnon**

BUDGET BUREAU

Don Tansley was asked if he found it difficult to make his own imprint on the Budget Bureau.

"No, I didn't really. The fact is (and it stemmed directly from Mr. Douglas himself, reinforced by Mr. Fines) they were always open to new ideas regardless of the source. They didn't judge an idea by the position it came from and I think this is quite unique.

"This is pure Tommy Douglas—to promote that kind of atmosphere where you felt free to put forth fresh ideas. And it became infectious. Nobody looked for credit, they looked for solutions."

⓪ **Don Tansley**

TOMMY KEPT HIS WORD

John Shaw had been trained as a civil servant in Britain. In Saskatchewan, he worked for the provincial government. He was a quiet Scot, with an illustrious war record; he was deeply religious and politically neutral. He was secretary of the Provincial Mediation Board when I was with the Board. Because of his heart trouble, I picked him up every morning on the way to work.

The only time he ever mentioned politics was on the morning following the 1952 election. "Tommy did it again," he said, as he slowly got into the car. Then he told me his story, for the first and only time.

After the 1944 election he expected to be dismissed, as he had been in 1929. He viewed the new Public Service Commission, instituted by the CCF government, with cynical suspicion. When he was called in for a review of his duties and salary, he fully expected this was the method that would be used to dismiss him. Three months later he was called back: his salary was dramatically increased and made retroactive to the date the CCF had been elected.

That morning in 1952, John Shaw recalled that Tommy Douglas had said he would treat civil servants fairly, that there would be no political favoritism and, John Shaw said, "He kept his word."

John Shaw never discussed politics with me again.

✍ **Ed Whelan**

IN THE NORTH

From 1950 to 1961, I worked as a field supervisor in the North for the Department of Natural Resources. As the only road into the north in 1950 was to La Ronge, I was issued a small aircraft. On one occasion we took Mr. Douglas on a day's trip to several communities, to annual meetings of local co-operative stores. The flight began at Emma Lake then to Ile-a-la-Crosse to Buffalo Narrows to La Loche to Pinehouse, to La Ronge and to Prince Albert.

At La Loche, Mr. Douglas saw an example of a settlement of several hundred people with hardly any visible means of support. We advised him that this community originated in the early fur trade days of the 19th century as it was at the south end of the "long portage" between the Churchill and McKenzie watersheds.

On the way to La Ronge for refueling, I radioed ahead that the Premier was on board. When we landed, there must have been 200 school children clustered on and around the dock. As we left, I heard Mr. Douglas say, "Think of the educational needs here for the next generation."

✍ **W. Earl Dodds**

AFFIRMATIVE ACTION

While Tommy was Minister of Health, I was a patient at Fort San. Despite the risk of catching tuberculosis, Tommy visited all the wards and treated us to one of his delightful stories.

Just before leaving our ward he suggested if we were ever in need of a job, we should give him a call. We said "thanks," but deep inside we had doubts of ever leaving the sanatorium alive.

I had been out of the San for nearly three years, and had travelled across the country looking for work. When I mentioned where I had spent five years of my life, I was told that they would keep my name on file and they would call me. In desperation, I dropped Tommy a note.

I got a job in the Purchasing Agency. Every time Tommy had occasion to visit E.T. Stinson, he would inquire about my health and how I liked my job. I loved my job, and gradually met many other ex-patients, some in wheelchairs, who had been given a chance by Tommy Douglas.

✍ **Veronica Eddy Brock**

CCF CIVIL SERVANT

As the war drew to an end in 1944, Tommy came to the camp where I was located and told me that he expected the CCF would win the upcoming election. He asked me to consider going into the civil service, not as a politician but as an administrator. "I have lots of people to tell me what to do but no one to tell me how to do it. I would want you to stay absolutely out of politics." This advice I followed to the letter as long as I was in the civil service.

✍ **Roy Borrowman**

Humanity First: CCF Programs

SASKATCHEWAN FIRSTS

When the CCF came to power in 1944, Saskatchewan was one of the poorest provinces in Canada, with the highest per capita debt; its institutions and services were worn out or non-existent.

Tommy Douglas and his government brought in advanced and innovative legislation that we have long taken for granted. Most of it started in the first term and was added to in the years that followed. Many of the following programs are "Saskatchewan Firsts"—first in Canada, first in North America.

◆ Ambulance plane.
◆ Hospitalization. Before this you couldn't get into hospital if you couldn't pay.
◆ Free treatment for Cancer, Tuberculosis, Venereal Disease, Polio.
◆ Free medical, dental, hospital services and drugs for: old age pensioners and their dependents, blind pensioners, mother's allowance cases, wards of the government, those receiving social welfare.
◆ Construction grants to communities to build hospitals.
◆ Budget Bureau to plan delivery of government programs.
◆ Radio broadcasts from the Legislature. Hansard made available.

◆ Trade Union Act: the right to bargain collectively; compulsory check-off; unfair labour practices defined; conciliation in disputes.
◆ Holidays with pay.
◆ The 8-hour day, 44-hour week for most employees.
◆ New, separate Department of Labour.
◆ Collective bargaining for government employees. Employment in government based on merit. Government employees allowed to participate in politics.
◆ Saskatchewan Government Insurance: low-cost automobile insurance.
◆ Equalization of education costs and opportunities. Grants to provide province-wide minimum education standards. Higher minimum teachers' salaries.
◆ New Department of Co-operation and Co-operative Development.
◆ Saskatchewan Bill of Rights.
◆ Saskatchewan Arts Board.
◆ Right to vote to 18-year olds.

RURAL POWER, ROADS, WATER

I was 16 years old in 1944 and I remember Tommy Douglas talking about a ten year plan to electrify rural Saskatchewan; that actually happened between 1946 and 1956.

W.J. Patterson, the Liberal premier, said at the time that this was impossible, as all farmers wanted was a windmill to pump water and a windcharger to provide light. Besides, it was impossible to get any company to put power into the farms as they were too far apart, and no company could get a return on their investment in two years, so it wouldn't be done.

Tommy said it could as all we had to do was to set up a company of our own and do it ourselves.

This was the beginning of modern farms as we understand them today. Think for a minute what it meant in the late 1940s and early 1950s to have an electric refrigerator replace the "dumb waiter" or ice box, electric washing machine, vacuums, stoves and, in the farm yards, lights in every building, yes, those prairie sentinels—the yard lights.

Later on in the 1950s, Tommy's government developed a plan to put water into virtually every farm, with a program for wells,

Tommy Douglas and Mayor J.H. Staveley turn on the valve to start Weyburn's natural gas distribution system, August 1958.

trenching, water pressure systems and pump outs at cost.

This was the final touch to the kind of amenities that only city people and the odd wealthy farmer had before.

By the late 1950s the farmer was using automatic waterers, electric welders, along with every line of other equipment.

Farm living was now into the 20th century, thanks to the foresight of Tommy and his government.

✍ **Alvin Hewitt**

CO-OP PHILOSOPHY

April 30, 1948, a North Battleford resident wrote to Mr. Douglas saying, "Your government is always ready and willing to help the Co-ops more so than the private firms. . . . I do not mind you giving the Co-ops a break at all . . . but I do think that firms such as I work for, also including our little hatchery business . . . should be entitled to the same treatment."

On May 6, 1948, Mr. Douglas replied: "It was very kind of you to take the trouble to write me, and I appreciate it very much. . . .

"The Co-operatives are the only way that large numbers of people can band together to protect themselves against monopolies which try to hold them up, either in the prices of things they buy, or on what they have to pay for services they require. For instance, we have given assistance to the farmers to help them set up their own implement co-operative. I think that over the years, the result of this will be to make the four big implement companies . . . bring their prices down to a reasonable level, just as the Government Insurance Office has forced insurance companies to be more moderate in their rates.

"Secondly, we haven't neglected small businesses; we have set up an Industrial Development Fund to give financial assistance to small businesses and people who want to start new industries. . . . In addition, we have set up a Trade Services Branch . . . for the purpose of assisting small businessmen by getting for them information about sources of raw material and potential markets. One objective of the CCF is to protect our people against monopolies by a three-fold plan:

1. Assisting small businessmen
2. Assisting co-operatives
3. By operating public utilities such as power, bus transportation, etc. . . . "Thank you again for writing."

SAB **Douglas Papers**

POWER

I first voted for Tommy Douglas in the summer of 1944 (voting for Gladys Strum) when I was in France after being Overseas for three years amid senseless slaughter and killing. And how elated I was when I heard that the CCF had won the election in Saskatchewan.

But they still had to prove themselves which they did many times over. Two of the greatest things that happened were the road improvement and the distribution of electricity to the farms.

So we were able to get to Moosomin which was 30 miles away on decent roads. And also to Regina and Brandon.

What a godsend that was when the Power came into the yard. We had a windmill to pump water for 60 head of cattle and 100 pigs; the wind hadn't blown for two weeks,- the only time it ever happened in Saskatchewan!

So when they switched the Power on about 9:00 in the morning on the 11th of January, 1956, I hooked up the team and sleigh and drove to Walpole five miles away, bought a pump jack and an electric motor. The cattle didn't get watered till the afternoon after I got it installed.

✍ **Hugh Ramage**

ELECTRIFICATION

Talk of the power coming to the farms was exciting. I shall never forget when we were able to "turn it on" at our farm. Ernest had polio that fall and was bedridden. We had cows and chickens so quite a few chores to do and cows to milk. When I could turn on the yard light, walk to the barn and turn on the light in the barn, have lights on in the house to come back to,- without the chimneys on the lamps all being black (we had Aladdin lamps), no more lanterns to clean and light,-the lamps could be put away.

Ernest (in bed) could turn on a light and read if he wished, and it made my load so much lighter!

✦ **Alice Walter**

OIL AND GAS EXPLORATION

There was a meeting in New York City about 1950. Douglas was the main speaker, to explain what the new government of Saskatchewan's policy would be in regard to investment in oil and gas exploration. It was arranged that Leonard Brockington would introduce him. (The first president of the CBC, Brockington was famous for his eloquence.)

Brockington made reference to various other oil producing countries of the world, and referred to the instability of governments there, the unpredictability and the risk that people took in investing.

He said, "Saskatchewan is perhaps an unknown quantity to all of you people,

but its participants are not unknown to me. I am here to tell you that I know Tommy Douglas, by reputation, by performance. When you deal with him about his oil and gas territories, you are going to deal with the toughest guy in the world. But, when he strikes a bargain, he will keep his word."

✦ **H.S. (Tim) Lee**

Tommy Douglas drops the puck at the Weyburn Colosseum for an exhibition game between Weyburn Redwings and Brandon Wheat Kings, October 21, 1961.

Irma, Shirley, Tommy and Joan Douglas at the CCF National Convention, Winnipeg, August 1948.

DUTY OF DIRECTORS

In talking to officials of co-ops and credit unions, Tommy stressed the fact that the primary duty of directors was to protect the interests of the members. The Department, he said, should never lose sight of its primary duty to encourage people to solve their own problems through co-operative enterprise, to do that rather than run things for them. He stressed the Department's services at co-op meetings, representing the whole community spectrum.

⊛ **B.N. (Barney) Arnason**

TOMMY DOUGLAS

. . . Equality in living and in health
Take precedence of privilege's wealth.
Insurance, power, oil and medicine,
When disciplined fell quickly into line!
Our Douglas, though opposed on every hand
Cut down a few Goliaths in the land. . . .

✂ **J.F. McKay**

Seminarian and the CCF

When I was a seminarian in Toronto, I was asked in a philosophy class to give details of the philosophy of the CCF in Saskatchewan and some of the programs they had initiated. This was in 1949. Some of the seminarians were quite impressed with the fact that here was a Catholic boy from Saskatchewan who was a member of the CCF.

In later years, because of the commitment of Mr. Douglas to Medicare, I became further involved with the CCF to the point where I spoke on public platforms. I was particularly incensed at the attitude of the medical doctors. Again, I felt very strongly that the sick were being badgered by lawyers and doctors to pay their bills, as our own family was, and here was universal Medicare which would take away all anxiety, and we had a group of reactionary people like the doctors trying to turn back the clock. This made me not just a member of the NDP but an active member. I spoke for various candidates on various platforms.

☸ **Fr. Isidore Gorski**

Tommy Douglas visits Canadian Army Hospital in Holland, 1945.

Hospitalization, January 1st, 1947

Tommy could be very, very rough when he wanted to move ahead and others were not moving. One story I've heard, and it's probably apocryphal, is about getting the program launched for hospital insurance. January 1st, 1947 was the set date. It was alleged that people said to him in November, "We're exceedingly sorry, but we won't be able to get this program going by January 1st, 1947."

To which Tommy is alleged to have said, "I'm really sorry to hear that. I'm really sorry, because the program is going to start on January 1st, 1947, and I've enjoyed working with you, but I guess we won't be working together again."

Thereupon, I gather, hospitalization got going.

☸ **Allan E. Blakeney**

CO-OP DAY

I have learned that the Lieutenant Governor of your Province, on the advice of the Government has proclaimed the 24th instant as "Saskatchewan Co-operative Day"...

No country, province or state in the world, so far as I know, has made such an outstanding recognition of the value and importance of the Co-operative movement. Even in Britain, where probably more than half the population are directly interested in the movement ... a "Co-operative Day" has not yet been officially proclaimed.

I note that your Premier makes an appeal in favour of the Movement 'to business, labour and professional groups', as well as to co-operators. Even though a person's interests may at the present time be competitive and profit motivated, it is quite possible for him philosophically, to be a co-operator...
SAB **Douglas Papers**
(*Note: George Keen, General Secretary, Co-operative Union of Canada, to B.N. Arnason, August 9, 1951.*)

Tommy Douglas at the official opening of the Co-op store in La Loche, 1959. Tommy, president Bobby Fontaine, Fr. Matthews.

MUTUAL AID FUND

Tommy was eleven years Minister of Co-operatives and Co-operative Development, 1950-1961, and I was his deputy minister. Although a small department it served a tremendous number of people; half the population were members of some form of co-op. Establishing the Department proved how important the co-operative-credit union movement was to the province, that the movement had come of age.

One thing did a lot for the co-op movement particularly the co-op credit sector,- sponsoring legislation to set up the Credit Union Mutual Aid Fund in 1953.

There had been a series of defalcations about 1950. Tommy received delegations of credit union and co-op leaders to discuss the need for legislation to set up a guaranteed reserve fund, to ensure that credit union members did not lose their deposits or investments.

He was able to convince them to widen the scope of the proposed fund so that it could be used to guarantee and reimburse members of credit unions sustaining losses in the past as well as the future.

He reminded members of the delegation that when he had been an MP there had been some discussion about the need for a special reserve fund for the chartered banks.

He agreed to make recommendations for credit union legislation based on his knowledge of the history of the banking system.

I have always felt that this was one of the main contributions that Tommy made in strengthening co-op legislation, the first of its kind in Canada now in effect across Canada.

✍ **B.N. (Barney) Arnason**

FIRST CLASS CITIZENS

If I love any man—and I'm speaking in the greater sense of love—it has to be Tommy Douglas. He made first class citizens out of us in Saskatchewan. Before that time, we always looked upon the East and said, "There's where it is. There's where the money is, there's where the opportunities are. We don't have much chance in Saskatchewan."

After Tommy came, we had all his schemes put in. We could now hold our heads up and say, "We're just as good as anyone. We can take our place with anybody."

✍ **Roy Borrowman**

WINDCHARGERS

We were talking about rural electrification. It's one of the anecdotes that you think about when power was being brought in. Tommy's old foe, Jimmy Gardiner, was holding forth at Melville and saying, "This man has no economic sense whatever. In the farm areas we can't afford to bring power in. I've had a windcharger on my farm for years, and it's quite ample. We don't need anything more than that."

Tommy was also at a meeting in Melville and they were questioning him.

"Why can't we get by with windchargers? Jimmy Gardiner says your idea is too expensive."

"Well," Tommy said, "possibly it's expensive and possibly the windchargers will work. But you aren't always going to have Jimmy Gardiner around to supply the wind."

✍ **Eiling Kramer**

The CCF government established Air Ambulance service in 1946, a year before hospitalization insurance for all citizens began.

THE AIR AMBULANCE

I had polio in 1946 when I was 12 years old. I got polio at Lake Alma, Saskatchewan and the only clinic at that time was in Saskatoon. We flew in the air ambulance to Saskatoon. It was a mild day in late November and the men in the town had to run alongside the plane to get it off the ground.

On the way to Saskatoon, between Regina and Moose Jaw, the plane quit, started to go towards the ground. My dad was really worried. Before it crashed we got going again.

Later Julian Audette, the pilot, explained: on those old Norseman planes there were two gas tanks, when the one in use got low, there would be a warning sound, and the co-pilot would switch to the other tank. They must have been talking or something and didn't notice the warning.

During the flight my dad worried about finances because he was just a Wheat Pool grain agent at Lake Alma and didn't have a lot of money. He was worried about paying the hospital bills and was very relieved when the hospital people told him that the treatment for polio had been made free, just about that time, one of Tommy's innovations, and it was a great relief to us.

⊛ Stan Oxelgren

Tommy Douglas visits College Mathieu, Gravelbourg, 1960.

Watershed for Catholics

I think the change in the attitude in the church regarding the NDP occurred roughly in the late 1950s and the early 1960s. It changed, simply, around the Medicare crisis here in Saskatchewan. After that Medicare crisis I was not the only Catholic clergyman who voted CCF or NDP. There were a good number of them. And today, I dare say, most of the Catholic clergymen vote NDP. And that change also occurred among the Catholic people. After all, the Papal Encyclicals said that the people had the right to health services.

I would say that the watershed was Medicare.

Fr. Isidore Gorski

Tommy and the Bishop

Tommy Douglas became Premier of Saskatchewan the same week that I became Bishop of Saskatoon, and he was talking about hospitalization. That was my first problem. He would come to see me with regard to hospitalization and together we worked out a plan for the Catholic hospitals. Education was a problem as well. Premier Douglas co-operated with me in everything that I asked him in the field of education. I have never—in Saskatoon, Winnipeg or Toronto—had a premier who co-operated with me as well as Tommy Douglas did.

Archbishop Philip Pocock interviewed by Dennis Gruending

E.C. (Ed) Morgan, archivist, in the stack area, Saskatchewan Archives, Regina, where the Papers of the Hon. T.C. Douglas are stored. Mr. Morgan catalogued the Papers and prepared the finding aid. This collection covers the years 1944-1961.

SMALL CLAIMS COURT — ANOTHER FIRST

In a Cabinet meeting we were talking about streamlining the Small Debts Act. Tommy wanted to know why this Act wasn't available for people who had damage claims, as well as debts. There really wasn't any answer to that. So we introduced the first Small Claims Court in North America.

　　　　✦ **R.A. (Bob) Walker**

SASKATCHEWAN ARCHIVES

Premier Douglas went to Saskatoon and had a chat with A.S. Morton and Dr. Simpson (George W. Simpson, head of History department, University of Saskatchewan), and Simpson said, "If you're going to have a country or province that's going to remember what it was like and do better because of it, you've got to establish an Archives, and when I say "Archives," I mean not only the things you pick up and keep, but a consistent record of everything that governments do and what corporations do and everything else, so we can make a fair assessment later on."

Douglas said to Simpson, "You set it up, how you think it might start." Simpson set it up and was the first Archivist.

The Saskatchewan Archives Act in 1945 was the first modern act in Canada—how to run an Archives and what the policy should be.

　　　　✦ **John H. Archer**

MENTAL HEALTH A PRIORITY

As a staff member from 1950 to 1971, I witnessed the sweeping reforms at the Saskatchewan Hospital, Weyburn, when Tommy Douglas was Premier.

One of his priorities was to reform the province's mental hospitals. The largest of these was located in the heart of his own constituency at Weyburn.

Renamed the Saskatchewan Hospital, the Weyburn institution was impressive. Well manicured lawns and beautiful gardens complimented the stately brick building. But its appealing exterior was deceptive. Designed for less than 500 beds when it opened in 1922, the hospital was bursting at the seams with more than 2,500 patients by 1944. After fifteen years of depression and wartime neglect, adequate treatment was provided for less than one-third of its patients. The remainder were condemned to a monotonous routine of custodial care; of the latter over 300, considered hopeless, were relegated to wards in the unfinished basement.

At the end of the Second World War, Tommy's government purchased the barrack blocks and administrative buildings of a military airport on the outskirts of Weyburn, which was developed into the Saskatchewan Training School. In 1946 a large number of mentally retarded patients were transferred here from the Saskatchewan Hospital reducing the population to just under 2,000. This was the beginning of better times for the patients and staff.

A prominent figure in Tommy's plans for change at the Weyburn Mental Hospital was Dr. Humphrey Osmond, a brilliant English psychiatrist and researcher, who was appointed superintendent in 1953. (Working closely with Dr. Osmond was Saskatchewan native, Dr. Abram Hoffer.)

Dr. Osmond tackled his new job with tremendous energy and imagination. His first concern was to raise the self-esteem of the overworked and demoralized nursing staff. Their training course was enriched and salaries increased; more importantly, the ward administration was changed from an authoritarian format.

Osmond gathered about him a strong team of social scientists who came from across North America and Europe. He was a tireless researcher into the causes of schizophrenia, the enigmatic disorder afflicting most of his patients. Dr. Osmond demonstrated that when their environment was improved even the most regressed patients would respond positively.

The media was attracted to Dr. Osmond and accounts of his work were published across Canada. As a result, visitors came to the Saskatchewan Hospital at Weyburn in great numbers. So many volunteered to help that a special department was established to co-ordinate their services.

In 1955, a million dollars worth of new construction was completed on the hospital grounds, including a nurses' residence and a modern treatment centre for mentally ill people in Saskatchewan suffering from tuberculosis.

In retrospect, probably one of the greatest contributions made during the Douglas era was to focus public attention upon the plight of the mentally ill in Saskatchewan and, indeed, throughout Canada.

✍ **Charles (Chuck) Bruce**

Tommy at the 1960 opening of the Saskatchewan Transportation Co. (STC) bus depot in Regina.

EQUAL OPPORTUNITY

Douglas was explaining the merits of equalization of school grants. He said, "It is just as important to all of us that the young fellow in Meadow Lake get as good an education as in Regina or Rosetown."

A trustee objected, he could see no reason why he should pay taxes to educate someone out of his own district.

Tommy's reply was, "Look, it is just as important that the young fellow in Meadow Lake get a good education as your children and mine—after all, he may come down to Regina, or Weyburn or Rosetown and marry your daughter or mine—and one dunce in the family is quite sufficient."

✍ **W.A. (Wes) Robbins**

FREEDOM OF INFORMATION

Douglas was the first man to offer his papers to the Archives. It was quite something for a cabinet minister to say, "We'll put them in the Archives."

"What about if people want to use them?"

"Well, you can set your own terms, and you can say what should be closed in the public interest, not in yours."

Tommy said, "That's right, and let's go further and say everything is open to the public after such a date. Set the rules now, we're not always going to be the government."

Tommy understood the importance of freedom of information.

☸ **John H. Archer**

NOBODY ELSE

I was thinking about Tommy bringing in the Hospital Act and hospital insurance in 1947. I remember him saying one time, "I wouldn't want to go through that again. It pretty nearly killed me." You don't just pass an act and put in hospital insurance. He had to talk to people, he had to plead, you know, and explain over and over, and just go, go, go, to get people to understand.

Nobody else in political life would have done it.

✦ **Percy Brown**

Tommy Douglas with Jimmie James, W. G. Davies and Howard Conquergood, at 1951 SFL Annual Convention, Moose Jaw, Sask.

ROCK IN A STORM

Tommy sympathized with the aspirations of the labour movement.

I was fortunate to have the opportunity to spend a few months in Regina just after Tommy and his government had the courage to bring in the first Medicare program. As you know, at the time the press in Saskatchewan was almost unanimously opposed to Medicare, and was fighting it, with the doctors who called the strike to try to scuttle the Bill. I was asked to come in by provincial labour to try to counteract the anti-Medicare and anti-government propaganda that was being spread about. I was very impressed by the way Tommy handled that controversial, emotional issue. I don't think anyone else, anyone political, could have lead the government and the province through that stormy time.

Tommy always maintained his arguments for Medicare. He was a rock in a storm.

✦ **Ed Finn**

SFL BRIEF

I believe it was in 1948. I was part of the delegation to present the annual brief of the Saskatchewan Federation of Labour to the government. Bill Davies organized a delegation of 120 people, so there was no meeting room large enough to accommodate them in the Legislative Building, except the Legislative Chamber. And so Tommy had the Chamber opened and they brought in more chairs.

The Cabinet sat on the floor of the House and we sat in the chairs that MLAs would sit in. I sat in Clarence Fines' seat,- the name tags were there. During the course of the presentation I got up several times to defend the brief and present additional arguments. And after the meeting, we had two or three hours. Tommy met and shook hands with people; he came to me and congratulated me. "Some day, Walter, you will be occupying this seat."

When I was Minister of Finance, I sat in the seat next to it.

✦ **Walter E. Smishek**

Tommy Douglas addresses a conference of treaty Indians, Valley Centre, Fort Qu'Appelle, Saskatchewan, October 30, 1958.

BILL 45 GIVES
INDIANS THE VOTE

Starting in 1945, in addition to correspondence, Tommy Douglas held a series of consultations with Band Chiefs to discuss their concerns. One of the main topics was extension of the franchise. This was opposed by some of these most influential leaders.

Resolutions at several annual CCF conventions recommended that all Indians have the right to vote in Saskatchewan elections.

Late in 1959 at the Provincial Council meeting Thora Wiggins of Prince Albert moved a resolution, which I seconded, that the Indians be given the vote without further delay. There was heated discussion. MLAs who had reservations in their constituencies were hesitant and advised against it, but the majority supported the Wiggins resolution.

Tommy said, "If that's the way you want it, that's the way it will be." Saskatchewan Indians living on reservations voted for the first time in the June 8, 1960 provincial election, Bill 45 having been assented to on March 14, 1960.

✍ **Ed Whelan**

◆ 4 ◆

From Buena Vista to Vancouver Island ◆ 1961-1971

Tommy Douglas was the federal leader of the New Democratic Party from 1961 to 1971. During that time the Party contested four general elections. In addition Tommy faced two personal by-election campaigns.

It was during these years that Tommy truly became a national figure. He campaigned constantly; he spoke in every corner of the country; he was a dominant figure in House of Commons debates.

Of Parliament Tommy once said, "One of the things I tried to do when I was in politics—and particularly in the House of Commons, where it can get pretty dull for long weeks and months on end, was to try to retain my sense of humour." He did and he enlivened Parliament in the process.

But most of the business of Parliament was serious. Tommy spoke on all of the important issues, sometimes taking unpopular stands, sometimes advancing a position ahead of the times. He spoke on civil liberties, international relations, Canada's obligation to the Third World and economic nationalism.

What Tommy said in the House is on record. What follows are anecdotes of people who remember Tommy or worked with him during those hectic years.

A Douglas for Me

The New Democratic Party founding convention took place in Ottawa in 1961, Monday to Friday, July 31 to August 4. It was a tremendous convention, - 2,083 registered delegates plus visitors and media, in Ottawa's Coliseum.

With the distinctive delegate badge, banners, posters, hats and music on many occasions, the gathering was almost exotic, more lively and colourful than the usual strictly business CCF convention.

It was the largest political convention that had ever been held in Canada and the first that was bilingual. Listening to the translation on headphones, and looking up at the person in the booth whose voice we heard, illustrated that ours is a nation with two official languages. There were signs and posters in French, as well as English, and more than 300 Quebec delegates. An Ottawa paper referred to the "crowds of spectators" in the public galleries.

There was the redoubtable Charlotte Whitton, mayor of Ottawa, in her official capacity. There was the large stage, easily seen from anywhere in the hall, across which streamed dignitaries including British Labour Party Leader Hugh Gaitskill, and Canadian trade union leaders imparting by their presence the change to the "New Party."

There was the exemplary chairmanship of Professor George Grube. There was the CBC-TV and radio gondola suspended from the roof. In the press room was the largest number of typewriters I had ever seen in one place.

And everywhere, almost palpable, tension built to the choice of leader. On Friday, the fourth day of the convention, the vote for

Tommy Douglas registers for the founding convention, Ottawa, August 1961. His delegate's badge is pinned on as Irma Douglas watches. The sign indicates which delegates report to this table.

Tommy was decisive—delegates carried him through the hall singing, *A Douglas For Me . . .*

Tommy became our federal leader at the age of 56. During the ten years of his leadership he displayed the energy, humour, inspiration and integrity we in Saskatchewan knew so well. Many of us were most reluctant to let Tommy go, we wanted him to stay in Saskatchewan, but I have never regretted the convention's choice.

✍ **Pemrose Whelan**

Joe Glazier and Tommy Douglas leading the singing of "This Land is Your Land" at the NDP founding convention, Ottawa, August 1961.

Pemrose Whelan, Howard McCurdy, Sheila Scott, and Peter Howe at the Regina delegates' table at the founding convention of the NDP in Ottawa, August 1961.

INDIVIDUALS AS INDIVIDUALS

His genius and geniality, his sense and sensitivity, his passion and his power have won for him admiration and respect wherever he went. Few indeed are those among us, regardless of political belief, who did not feel proud when Tommy Douglas spoke for Saskatchewan.

But maybe the real picture of a man isn't that which emerges from his contact and influence with large groups of people. Certainly it isn't just that. Certainly it's also, perhaps more accurately, the way in which individuals react to him as individuals.

He'll listen—he'll try to explain, if possible to rectify. And it will all be done with warmth and sensitivity and sincerity. It will be done in that way because of his profound conviction that each individual human being is important.

The same concern for people, individual people, is reflected in his care of their written requests. It may well be that history will record this established integrity in dealing with individuals as individuals as the greatest reason for his political success.

✂ **Woodrow S. Lloyd**

Woodrow Lloyd and Tommy Douglas arriving at the annual convention of the Saskatchewan CCF at the Trianon in Regina, 1961.

ALWAYS A REALIST

Tommy had a sense of realism about politics. I think also he had a tremendous amount of courage to take on unpopular causes when he knew they were right.

He knew when he took on the national leadership that it was going to be an uphill struggle. I don't think too many people at his age, and having accomplished all he had in Saskatchewan, would have taken on that tremendous extra burden at that time in his career. But Tommy took it on.

☿ **Ed Finn**

Money for Armaments

During the years of the Great Depression, hopelessness and despair prevailed. Many people actually went hungry. The entire social and economic structure stagnated.

A few years ago I heard Tommy Douglas describing those conditions and the general mood of the times.

As Douglas pointed out, the misery and suffering didn't stem from widespread shortages of food and other essentials. Quite the contrary. Huge surpluses, particularly of foodstuffs, continued to pile up in the storehouses. The problem was how to get these items into the hands of those who needed them. The stock answer was always the same—there was no money. Then in the late summer of 1939 Adolph Hitler unleashed Germany's potent war machine, dragging the world into conflict. Douglas recalled the tense moments in the House of Commons. Having dispensed with the formalities of going to war the House turned its attention to funding the project. In just 15 minutes MPs voted $1 billion, an extremely large sum in those days. A few days later, more billions of dollars were made available.

How astonishing, Douglas marvelled. For years Parliament had steadfastly refused to consider furnishing the relatively small amounts needed to alleviate the worst effects of the Depression. Then in a few minutes, the MPs suddenly discovered a whole $1 billion.

Alas, that no longer seems to be the case. As our economy unfolds it reveals many characteristics associated with the Great Depression. Again, we are hearing the refrain—echoes from the past. There isn't enough money to provide everyone with such basic essentials as health care, housing, food and education.

Ah, but we do have money for armaments. Even though enough weaponry already exists to annihilate contemporary civilization, we slavishly follow the lead of our war-minded neighbor to the south.

✂ **Arthur Turner**

United College - 1958

My first meeting with Tommy was in 1958. It was in the old United College auditorium in Winnipeg. United College in those days was a beehive of activity. We had a mock parliament,- the Liberals, the Conservatives, the CCF, Social Credit, Communist,- all five. As the United College CCF group we were successful in getting Tommy to speak. The auditorium was just packed, standing room only. You could hear a pin drop in that auditorium.

And it was the most moving speech I had heard. It had a very deep impression upon me. It was the first time I heard Tommy, one of the first speeches I heard from a major political leader. I was 18 or 19 and I can remember some of the Tory students coming up and just shaking their heads, and saying they were resisting coming over because of the strength of Tommy's logic. The strength of Tommy's oratory had such a moving impact upon them. I remember we were so proud as students that we had Tommy come to speak to the meeting.

⚙ **Howard Pawley**

TOMMY IN WATERLOO

I met Tommy about 1960 or 1961 when he came to speak at what was then called Waterloo Lutheran College, now Sir Wilfrid Laurier University. He had been invited by the political club. That was a most unprogressive part of Ontario. And the students were anything but New Democrats. But it was shortly after that the New Democratic Party, for the first time, formed the government in the mock legislature at the University. So Tommy certainly did us some good.

I think the impressive thing was Tommy's conviction that the need is for governments to act to help the people, rather than business.

It was sort of funny that although the New Democrats won that year there was real desperation because the small club didn't have enough people to even fill the seats they had won. So they came to people like me, who hadn't been active, to become members, and asked me to sit so they would have enough bodies to form the government!

⊛ **Alex Taylor**

NEVER HECKLE TOMMY

Decades ago, Norah, my wife, and I first heard Tommy Douglas speak to a crowd of rowdy young people in the old Winnipeg Auditorium. In four minutes he silenced the hecklers with his wit and wisdom. They then listened politely to his sprightly address. Though he failed to convert every member of that audience to his own political persuasions, he gained for all time their respect and admiration.

✂ **Ernie Mutimer**

WIT OF THE PARTY

I was the president of the Ottawa CCF Club. Stanley Knowles had just been elected and we were having a celebration up in the House of Commons. Mr. Coldwell and David Lewis and all the rest of the gang were there, and I was introducing Tommy to the gang, and proceeded to say that I had heard that he was the wit of the Party. Tommy's first words were these, "The chairman is only half right." It was a pretty good example of Tommy's ability to put down his own importance for the sake of a good laugh.

⊛ **Walter B. Mann**

THAT MAN MADE SASKATCHEWAN

When Tommy Douglas was leader of the Party at Ottawa, there was a nominating convention in Assiniboia. I was seated beside a gentleman about 80 years of age who was hard of hearing. Across the front of the stage were a lot of pictures of Tommy, large size. While the meeting was going on, he would say out loud to me, "That's the man that made Saskatchewan." I turned a deaf ear, so I didn't hear more but when they were counting the ballots I decided I would listen to what he had to say. He lived away down south of Assiniboia and he said, "If you weren't a Liberal you couldn't even get relief. You were nobody. You didn't dare open your mouth. But Tommy came and we became people."

⊛ **Hugh Alexander**

I Learned About Tommy

The reason I became political has to do with my Grade 6 Social Studies teacher in 1965. She told us one day about the doctors' strike in Saskatchewan upon the introduction of Medicare by Tommy Douglas.

I grew up in a poor family. We had some coverage under my father's employment but it wasn't full medical coverage. Seven kids on one low income was very tight.

And then to hear that the Liberals had conspired with the doctors, with the Saskatchewan Medical Association to get that strike engineered, to prevent Medicare coming into force just appalled me.

And then I learned all about Tommy.

I went home from school that day. My uncle was visiting from Greenland, my mother's brother. My mother had come home from work. My father was about to walk in, probably within five minutes. I turned to my mother and said, "Hi, Mom. Guess what? I'm a socialist now!" And my mother said, "That's nice." My uncle was very condescending and said, "Sure, sure, you'll grow out of it, it's a temporary affliction of youth." That made me angry and that is when I decided that, in the long term, I am going to do things. I'm not going to let him say that I am going to grow out of this.

Aside from Grant Notley, Tommy Douglas would have been the single greatest influence on my political perspective. Once I had discovered Medicare, I didn't stop reading, I read everything I could about Tommy Douglas and about Saskatchewan politics, and national politics, I combed newspapers. I practically memorized the Regina Manifesto. I started going to conventions, started listening.

Tommy's statement that means the most

Tommy Douglas joins a picket line for the printers' union in front of the Parliament Buildings, Ottawa, 1964.

to me is the one I keep on my fridge and it's been on my fridge close to 20 years.

Surely if we can produce in such abundance in order to destroy our enemies, we can produce in equal abundance in order to provide food, clothing and shelter for our children. If we can keep people employed for the purpose of destroying human life, surely we can keep them employed for the purpose of enriching and enhancing human life.

Just that really simple philosophy. If we have the resources to do bad things, obviously we have the resources to do good things.

◡ **Pam Barrett**

A Trip to Newfoundland

I had been elected leader of the party in Newfoundland at about the same time Tommy became federal leader. He came into Newfoundland a couple of times and did a tour of the Island with me and other Newfoundland New Democrats. Tommy could adapt to any audience whether they were farmers, labour, whether they were fishermen, by talking to them in their own terms, and he obviously enriched his lines with appropriate anecdotes, jokes that illustrated the points he wanted to make.

The first time I heard him give his simple allegory of the black cats and the white cats was in Newfoundland, at Corner Brook in a hall that was just about packed. People came out to hear Tommy. They came initially to hear him as a personality because of his reputation as a speaker, but they left impressed by the message he had to give, because the jokes and anecdotes were simply reinforcing and illustrating the main points he wanted to make.

As an orator I have never seen his like and never expect to see or meet anyone who could so capture an audience and hold their atten-

Tommy Douglas arriving in Vancouver on September 8, 1961 for the founding convention of the B.C. NDP.

tion. Time just seemed to have no meaning. He could speak, sometimes for an hour, and not a person moved, there was not a sound until they applauded. At times he could go 10 or 15 minutes in a serious vein, but speaking in such a way that he was able to hold their interest. I was captivated by him personally.

As well, he was so approachable, he never put forth any airs of superiority or exclusiveness.

✎ **Ed Finn**

1962 FEDERAL CAMPAIGN

Tommy became federal NDP leader in 1961 and ran in Regina in 1962. It was a very difficult campaign because of the Medicare issue. The American Medical Association and other enemies of Medicare moved into Saskatchewan. They had the backing of most of the press and the press came to Regina from everywhere. Accuracy didn't seem to matter. They zeroed in on Tommy Douglas as the instigator of Medicare. They used radio and television. Our canvassers were abused on the telephone and harassed on the doorstep. Doors were slammed so hard it is a wonder the frames didn't come off. Seasoned canvassers were demoralized and some gave up; the personal abuse worked.

I remember a call from the committee room about 7:45 one morning. Mrs. Kathleen Moore said, "There's a hammer and sickle painted on our door. What shall I do?" I said, "Around the corner there's a paint store; get some paint cleaner and clean the door as fast as you can. I'll be down right away."

When I got to the committee room, the door had been cleaned off, hammer and sickle were gone. Mrs. Moore asked, "Why did you insist on cleaning off the paint so fast?" I looked over my shoulder. There was *The Leader-Post* photographer. As he rounded the corner he aimed his camera at the door.

Ed Whelan, campaign manager; A.R. Ellis, returning officer; Tommy Douglas, candidate; and Lorne Pearce, official agent, at the signing of Tommy's nomination papers for the 1962 federal election campaign in Regina.

I said, "Do you want something?"

This was the kind of thing they were doing.

We were heading into an election where we would have great difficulty. Tommy lost. The Liberal candidate folded and the Conservative candidate walked in and beat us soundly; 22,200 to 12,700. Tommy said, "Well, I saved my deposit."

✍ **Ed Whelan**

I'll Fight Again

When Tommy ran federally in Regina in 1962, Ed, my husband, was campaign manager. I helped where I could and enjoyed accompanying Irma to daytime functions.

Election night when the results were known, Ed and I went to the TV station with Tommy and Irma. I stood off-camera when Tommy spoke with his characteristic dignity and courage. He concluded with:

Fight on, my men, said Sir Andrew Barton,
I am hurt, but I am not slain.
I will lay me down and bleed awhile,
And then I'll rise and fight again.

We left the TV station and drove to the Douglas home on Angus Crescent. Irma prepared tea and raisin toast. Tommy and Irma gave us each a gift in appreciation of our part in the campaign.

There was one long distance call from Eastern Canada. The door bell rang and the telegraph messenger (John Higginbotham), with tears in his eyes, handed a telegram to Tommy.

There were no more phone calls, there were no visitors.

In spite of his long service to the Province and his immense popularity, in defeat no one came near Tommy. It has since seemed to me one of the saddest possible comments on public life.

It was an evening I cannot forget.

✍ **Pemrose Whelan**

Humour in Defeat

Tommy used humour effectively to defuse the bitterness of defeat.

On election night in 1962 as results came into our headquarters in Hotel Saskatchewan, everyone was upset. Tommy was losing, badly. Even the CBC reporter had tears in his eyes when he interviewed Tommy.

A few days later Tommy met the Saskatchewan MLAs. He appeared relaxed. The faces of the MLAs were grim and worried, they were concerned for Tommy.

He said it could have been worse, the Liberals in Regina had lost their deposit, he had saved his. He recalled setbacks suffered by other parties in various elections, and by the CCF in the 1930s.

Tommy said it reminded him of something that had happened in Weyburn during the Depression. A summer hail storm hit the town and did a lot of damage.

The United Church board met in the church. As they shovelled hail stones from the floor, one member reported that, "every window is broken on this side." Another pointed out that, "we haven't money for plywood to cover the windows." A third said, "the floor is ruined, there are marks on the pews." There was silence until a man who hadn't spoken before blurted out, "You should see the Anglican Church; blew the roof right off!"

The MLAs laughed; the tension was broken.

✍ **Ed Whelan**

Tommy Douglas addressing the Canadian Labour Congress (CLC) convention in Toronto, 1968.
"I am here because I want people to know whose side I'm on."

THE BLUE HOUSE

I remember bringing him home to what I was proud to call my home, bringing him for lunch. We had ordered the decoration of the house from a faded (what we thought was faded) blue stucco piece of advertising stuff. It turned out that it was an intense blue colour. They used to say that Air Canada pilots found their way into the Ottawa Airport by observing the "blue house."

I had the top down on the car and Tommy in the seat beside me. We came around the corner and there was the house, and Tommy said, "Who in Heaven's name would paint their house that colour?" And I said, "Tommy, that's my house. That's where you are going to have lunch."

He said, "Get me one of your big knives and I will slit my throat."

I gather that Tommy used this afterwards when lecturing to candidates to be careful where they made comments.

✺ **Walter B. Mann**

TOMMY'S CONTRIBUTION

You have to look across the country and see how many provinces adopted what we did. Not perhaps because they loved it, but because they feared not to do it.

There are so many things that are deemed worthwhile and talked about that are never done. Tommy Douglas talked about things and did them.

✺ **W.G. (Bill) Davies**

Members of Federal NDP Women's Committee meet with Tommy Douglas. Back row: Pemrose Whelan, Peggy Prowse. Seated: Edith Cove, Eva Latham, Ina Brockelbank, and Tommy, Ottawa, 1965.

ACTION AND TENACITY

What was unusual about Tommy? What made him stand out among other men, women? What drove him?

His caring for people. He wasn't a man who carried his religion on his sleeve. Anything but. He believed in doing. I think that is the best way of putting it. Rather than just telling. Action was the thing that mattered to Tommy Douglas.

I think you have to admit that persistence is another thing—they tried to stop him many times but he didn't stop. Tenacity, I think, instead of persistence, is a more adequate term. But don't forget the time he was defeated here in Regina in 1962. He came right back and a lot of others would have quit and said the heck with it. That's it. He didn't.

⊛ **Eric McKay**

A QUICK DECISION

We rented Maple Leaf Gardens in Toronto in 1963. There was an immense crowd of about 15,000, the biggest political crowd anyone had had in Canada to that time. A man rushed up on the stage. He grabbed hold of Tommy's lapels. He shouted, "Not Douglas, but Trudeau." I was standing in the wings watching, and Tommy unmistakably gave him a couple of good jabs in the solar plexus, at which point this guy's hands released Tommy's coat. Donald Mac-Donald was chairman of the meeting. He and several other people hustled the man out of the hall.

Later, back at the hotel, I said to Tommy, "That was something, the way you smacked that guy in the guts." Tommy said, "Oh, I didn't." I said, "Of course you did, Tommy, I was watching." "Oh, no, I didn't." I said, "Not only was I watching but there was a CBC camera crew in the wings, they got a shot of the whole thing." And he said, "I had to make him let go of my lapels."

Tommy solved the problem quickly with that jab.

⊛ **Cliff Scotton**

David Lewis, Irma Douglas, Cliff Scotton and Tommy Douglas, Winnipeg, in 1970s.

FASHIONING A STORY

Tommy's stories always had that essential message which was simple but understandable to everybody. You could hear them over and over again and they still had a freshness and they still had a meaning.

I used to watch how Tommy would develop a story during the course of a campaign. Tommy told the story every night with just minor variations, in terms of timing and so forth. At the end of the week it was like someone getting a piece of wood or stone and fashioning it into something that was quite different and was complete and had symmetry and beauty. Tommy did this with a story.

⊛ **Cliff Scotton**

"I Want to Talk to These People"

I learned very early that Tommy was a demanding taskmaster. As a young junior, you would get mildly rebuked if the microphones or the platform wasn't quite in shape, if arrangements weren't on time.

One time, when he was federal leader, my job was to engineer a press conference, stand at the back of the hall and at an appropriate time step in and say, "Excuse me, ladies and gentlemen, Mr. Douglas has another appointment."

On one occasion Tommy's admonition to me was, "Every once in a while if I get hung up with someone, I would like you to gently say we've got to move on."

I found invariably if things were going well, Tommy just said, "No, no, no, forget about that, I want to continue and answer questions."

The same thing would happen in a crowd when he was meeting people. He'd say, "I want to talk to these people."

Tommy and Irma Douglas going into a rally in Winnipeg, March 1965.

Afterwards, I'd ask him, "Did I move too quickly." "You have to move me along, but you have to understand also that I've got to make my point." He wanted to get his message out.

And there was a certain temperament there that was difficult to fathom in some ways. You'd do what he wanted you to do, but you weren't quite sure that you'd pleased him.

⚙ **Roy Romanow**

A Matter of Good Timing

During the mid-1960s as Federal NDP Leader, Tommy, from time to time, made the two-hour train trip from Ottawa to Montreal. In Montreal, unless the event was to be televised, it was assumed that a political meeting would begin half an hour after the announced time. This was explained to Tommy; he was told that if the meeting were to start on time either no one would be there, or people would be annoyed that the meeting got under way before they arrived. Tommy's response tended to be a short lecture on the virtue of punctuality.

Laurier LaPierre was to be nominated on May 17, 1967 for the 1968 federal election. Tommy agreed to attend. Notices were sent out stating that the meeting would start at 7:30 pm.

A special notice, however, went to Tommy in Ottawa, in which it was noted that the meeting would start at 8:00 pm.

After an audience with the Mayor and dinner with the local riding officials, Tommy arrived at the full hall. At exactly 8:00 pm the meeting got under way.

Tommy made a point of congratulating the somewhat bemused crowd on their punctuality and complimented the organizers, only some of whom knew about the two notices for this meeting.

As far as is known, Tommy never guessed at the kindly deception.

✍ **Richard Comber**

A Grassroots Social Democrat

After I got my law degree, I articled, and I practiced what Tommy Douglas preached, which is bringing equality and justice to the ordinary men and women of this world.

I set up a storefront lawyer program in Vancouver. I worked with citizens' groups to stop the freeways and urban renewal schemes that were going to destroy Gastown and Chinatown, and wipe out 1,200 homes through the east side of the city.

I represented the Chinese community as their lawyer. I also worked with a lot of welfare groups in the skid row, down town, east side, taking on crime and alcohol problems and the slum landlords. I acted on behalf of debtors, tenants, people fighting government bureaucracy.

It was good training to be a grassroots democrat and a fighter on behalf of ordinary men and women.

That's how I got on City Council. I got mad at City Hall because my communities were being pushed around by the arrogant right wing.

I'm basically a grassroots populist Social Democrat. A lot of that I learned from Tommy Douglas.

🜨 **Mike Harcourt**

TOMMY'S FRIENDS

I met Tommy at the airport to take him to the rally at the Regina Armouries in 1968. He had been speaking frequently and was tired. He said, "Have a taxi ready at the back of the hall. Get me out of there as soon as it's over so I can have a good night's sleep."

The Armouries was packed; 6,500 people stood up when he arrived, singing, *Tommy is Our Leader*. Tommy spoke. They were enthusiastic, they stood up, they interrupted him with applause and laughed loud and long at his jokes.

It was a great meeting and ended on a high note. Tommy's need for sleep vanished. When I said, "The cab is at the back, Tommy, the driver is waiting to drive you to the hotel," he looked at the audience and said, "I can't leave now. There's Eric Oxelgren. You know, he ran in Bromhead in 1934. He's an old friend, I can't go away and leave him." And he didn't. He stayed shaking hands with friends.

It was one of the largest and most enthusiastic meetings ever held in Regina. What had happened was that people who had voted against him in 1962 had come that night to say they had been wrong. The NDP won both seats in that 1968 federal election. The people of Regina voted for Tommy.

When we got to the hotel, Tommy apologized to the cab driver for holding him up and said he had run up quite a bill. The driver said, "This one is on me, Mr. Douglas."

Then Tommy attended the reception for the press, shaking hands and smilingly restating NDP policy. When he went to bed at midnight he didn't seem tired at all.

✍ **Ed Whelan**

Tommy Douglas accompanied by Tommy Shoyama in the 1960s.

HE MIGHT BE HUNGRY

We would be walking through a town, and a panhandler would come up. Tommy would hand him a $10 bill. I said, "Gracious, Tommy, that guy is just going to head for the pub with that." But he said, "He might be hungry too."

✌ **Alex McLellan**

LESSON IN GOVERNMENT

After meeting Tommy, I read up on the Saskatchewan CCF and the way that Tommy ran the government.

There are valuable lessons to be learned from Tommy Douglas in terms of chewing off digestible chunks of change, so that people don't get indigestion.

Get a mandate for that change before the election. Take it to the public and lay it up front: Here is the 10-point program, what we think needs to be done to improve our society. Here is what it will cost. Give us a four-year mandate. We'll do it and have a game plan for those four years.

Make sure you run a clean, efficient government that keeps its ear to the ground, that's always involved with people. Have a two-way dialogue and make sure you are sensitive to people, and their recommendations and criticism.

Ⓞ **Mike Harcourt**

FIGHT TO KEEP

Tommy had foresight. Twenty-five years ago, he told me there are three things that we always have to fight to keep: (1) The Crow Rate. (2) The Wheat Board. (3) Medicare.

Ⓞ **Hugh Alexander**

IN TRAINING

Tommy was one of the most disciplined people I have ever known. You talk about him having a boxing background, an athletic background. I have always thought he had a natural bent to be disciplined, but the athletic training was part of that.

In the election campaign he was just like an athlete getting ready for the Olympics. His food was completely disciplined. He had certain foods and that was all. He drank a certain amount of coffee and no more. He got a certain number of hours of sleep. He got up at the same time every morning. He had a certain breakfast every morning. We tried to follow most of his wishes, to see that campaign meetings ended at a certain time so that he could get back to his apartment. He didn't do what young campaigners, in my experience, would do; rehashing everything until two o'clock in the morning. When the meeting was over, Tommy would get back to the apartment. He might ask you to come in for some hot chocolate, or we might have stopped at a cafe.

Then you met again at seven o'clock in the morning when he was having breakfast. And that is when you discussed what had gone on the day before, after you had a chance to sleep on it and to make some good decisions about what needed to be done.

Ⓞ **Joyce Nash**

Sowing the Seeds

I spent four years as leader in Newfoundland and probably would not have gone more than a year without encouragement from Tommy.

One of the things I learned from him was that if what you were doing was worth doing, it was never a hopeless effort; there was always some measure of progress made even if, when you talked to a group of people, you only reached one or two of them. That was Tommy's message to me,- you are planting the seeds here, if may take years, it may take decades but eventually the new plant will take root and grow.

I thought of that message from Tommy the night that Fonse Faour was elected in Corner Brook, in the riding where I ran twice in the 1960s and where I got 4,000-5,000 votes, he was able to eventually win.

Fonse phoned me shortly after he was elected. He could not remember Tommy, he was too young at the time Tommy visited Newfoundland in the early 1960s, but he knew that Tommy had been there. Both, on the phone, in our own way, gave credit to Tommy for having come into the Island, inspiring a number of us to take up the struggle on the Island and to keep the flame bright there until finally the seeds planted in the 1960s bore fruit and we started to win some elections.

☯ **Ed Finn**

Talking Politics

I worked for the CPR in the summer when I was going to university in the 1960s. I met Tommy Douglas on the cross-country train. I was the first waiter in the dining room and had the privilege of serving him.

I told him I was a political science student, interested in politics. When the meals were finished he invited me to come back and sit and talk with him. And for three days, an hour here and there, we talked.

He was extremely easy to talk to and very gracious. Here was a national party leader taking the time to speak with a young college student, and he didn't know me at all.

At that time I wasn't involved politically. I had our generation's viewpoint that we had to create new political structures, that we had power of people, grassroots democracy, and that the existing political parties had become calcified, including the NDP.

But what Tommy said stayed with me. I read and I kept involved with Tommy's kind of commitment to ordinary people, from his Christian, social gospel roots, basically our family background. My mother was an active rebel in the United Church and implanted the message, "practice what you preach," as did Tommy.

My family were basically non-active Liberals from the prairies, big fans of Trudeau. They've voted NDP for the last 15 years. It didn't take me long to realize that the Liberal party talk a better fight than they actually do.

And I became committed, an active New Democrat in the fall of 1968, and have remained very active since. But it was Tommy Douglas who really pushed me over into being a New Democrat.

☯ **Mike Harcourt**

Tom Paulley (Winnipeg; son of Daisy and Russ Paulley) and Tommy Douglas, Port Elgin, Ont., during the NDP Women's Workshop, 1966.

FRANK SCOTT RATES TOMMY

Frank R. Scott quite unexpectedly paid him a compliment in a conversation in the 1970s. Looking back and comparing the first national leaders of the CCF-NDP, Scott said: "There was J.S. Woodsworth—philosophical, spiritual. M.J. Coldwell—the supreme parliamentarian, superbly good.

"But Tommy was it. Tommy related the whole thing to people, to every type of person. He was never very terrifying in his ideas even when putting forth bold CCF policy. And he was able to put into words that made it seem perfectly sensible and reasonable to ordinary people. And he was therefore the best."

✂ **Doris French**

STAYING IN SHAPE

The more personal, very relevant bit of advice I got was Tommy's concern for staying in shape, and he was a guy who was full of zip and energy and it wasn't accidental, and it wasn't a great mystery. It was because he looked after himself in terms of sleep, in terms of exercise and in terms of diet.

One time after I had been Leader of the Party for just a couple of years, coming back from an exhausting trip, I had a chat with him in the hall. Tommy, in his usual way, said, "Hi Ed, how did the trip to the West go?" I said, "It was great but I am tired." So this lead to a conversation about getting in shape and he in his nice, discreet way, said, "How do you eat?" So we chatted about that and then I asked, "How do you eat?"

He said, "Come to lunch with me." So I went and had lunch and I remember it very vividly. He had prunes and bran muffins and maybe one other thing for lunch that particular day. And I said, "Tommy, that's your lunch?" It was. That's it. So I joined him for lunch the next day, and he had prunes and bran muffins and whatever the third item was —I forget. I didn't join him the next day, but I asked him what he had and it was the same thing.

So I tried this Tommy Douglas lunch for about a week and I must frankly say I couldn't sustain myself as Tommy had done probably for 50 years up to that time, on that precise lunch of prunes and bran muffins.

I did learn the point and subsequently changed my eating habits considerably.

🜨 **Ed Broadbent**

Tommy Douglas, Walter Smishek, and Woodrow LLoyd at NDP picnic in Ogema, Saskatchewan, 1970.

A POLITICAL IDEAL

Mr. Douglas remains my political ideal. I don't think there will ever be another like him and I do believe the whole quality of Canadian political life has diminished with his passing.

However, I was really unaware of his existence prior to his becoming Premier of Saskatchewan, and all my contacts with the man have been in the context of attending meetings he addressed, and so shared by large numbers of people.

The only personal contact I had came at a dinner just prior to the founding of the New Democratic Party in 1961. My husband served as the chairman of the New Party committee here in Manitoba, so at a large dinner at the Fort Garry Hotel held to launch the project, we were at the head table. Tommy was the guest speaker and I was fortunate enough to be seated beside him.

In 1981, I ran as an unsuccessful candidate in the provincial election here. Mr. Douglas attended a rally in support of Andy Anstett during that campaign and I again had a chance to speak to him briefly. To my amazement he remembered me. The man must have had a phenomenal memory because the previous contact had been 20 years earlier.

✍ **Audrey Tufford**

MAN WITH A VISION

"Working on this play has made me realize that he [Tommy] fought against narrow-mindedness. . . . If people care about other people there isn't one problem in our society today that can't be resolved."

Such is the case in the play *Tommy*, which Bill Hugli says transcends partisan politics. "To break it down in its simplest terms I think it's how a man who has a vision of society copes with defeat and finds within himself the strength to carry on despite the defeat."

The original idea for the play was Hugli's. Almost two years ago, some people asked him to perform Tommy Douglas's famous Cream Separator speech at a New Democratic Party get-together.

✂ **Bill Hugli interviewed by Ed Schroeder**

You Can Make a Difference

In talking to Tommy, I said that I didn't think the old-line parties were up to what was needed in terms of dealing with the Vietnam War at that time and the great society changes in the United States: the poverty and civil rights and the freeing of people from colonialism and the changes that needed to take place.

Also, I was critical about the communist systems, that they were outdated.

Tommy said, "Well those issues are still there and the party of the people isn't going to work unless there is an organization behind it, and there is long-term commitment, and you're disciplined and learn to be patient, then, you can make a difference."

That's the key thing I learned.

You can make a difference in Canada, and you're not going to win all the time.

Tommy said, "Even if you don't get into government, you can make a difference," pulling out the examples of J.S. Woodsworth and Stanley Knowles and the voices of Angus and Grace MacInnis on behalf of the Japanese Canadians in 1942; and the impact we had in Saskatchewan in making the lives of the rural people so different; rural electrification, health insurance and all the practical changes we helped introduce.

I've never had a sense of cynicism, of "it's hopeless, you can't change things," because of Tommy's example.

It may be hard. It may be tough. There may be setbacks, but, you can make a difference.

☯ **Mike Harcourt**

Tommy and M.J. Coldwell in front of Parliament Buildings, Ottawa, in the 1960s.

Tommy's Attraction

He was such a powerful man, I think it came from a place very deep inside him. He attracted people, they were interested in getting near him to hear what he had to say. People understood that he felt for them, for everyone of them.

☯ **Janice Valecourt**

Tommy Douglas at microphone during a visit to Weyburn, 1970.

HIS FINEST HOUR

For Tommy Douglas there would be one last battle, in October 1970, the FLQ Crisis.

. . . One of the first voices raised in protest was the voice of Tommy Douglas.

. . . Despite his personal anguish Douglas held firm to his unshakable conviction that the War Measures Act was wrong. It was, perhaps, his finest hour. It was certainly his loneliest. But gradually the people came back to him, recognizing his courage and the rightness of his last great stand.

✂ **Donald Brittain**

WIDELY LOVED

Surely no man in Canadian public life has been more widely loved than Tommy Douglas. For some it was the tenacity, the audacity, that fought the medical establishment of Saskatchewan, backed by the Canadian Medical Association and the American Medical Association, for medicare for the people of his province and eventually for all of Canada.

For some it was because he actually did what he promised to do—confounding the politician-watchers. He checked off election promises like a conscientious shopper with the weekly spending allowance in his hand—and Saskatchewan got cheap car insurance, electrification for farms and villages, an efficient bus line that paid a surplus into the provincial treasury, the obstacles removed from co-operative growth, a moratorium on farm mortgage foreclosures in the years of crop failure. Let the bankers share the bad times and wait for their money as the farm housewife waits for her new stove, said Tommy Douglas.

Some loved him for his irreverent sense of fun, a gaiety of spirit that lightened the ponderous business of government and assured us that it was quite easy after all, and our world could indeed be a good and happy place.

I remember the playful jibe at an elder colleague, a craggy, raw-boned and unsmiling man, of whom he said: "Angus was never born, you know. Angus was quarried."

I remember his wonderful stories of black cats and white cats who took turns ruling Mouseland, and the temerity of the first little grey beast who dared to squeak: "Let's elect mice to Parliament."

✂ **Doris French**

◆ 5 ◆

British Columbia ◆ 1962-1979

Eighteen years after leaving the House of Commons to enter provincial politics, Tommy returned to Parliament as the MP for Burnaby-Coquitlam, one of the Vancouver ridings. Erhart Regier MP, originally from Saskatchewan, had just been re-elected in Burnaby-Coquitlam. Upset by Tommy's defeat in Regina, Regier resigned his seat hoping Tommy would succeed him. In the October 1962 by-election Tommy won handsomely. He was re-elected twice. However, in 1968, the year of Trudeaumania, Tommy lost by a few votes in Burnaby-Seymour.

That summer he agreed to run in another British Columbia riding, Nanaimo-Cowichan-The Islands where he was elected in a 1969 by-election. He represented the riding for 10 years. In total, Tommy was a British Columbia MP for 17 years, until he left public life in 1979.

In Burnaby, Irma and Tommy lived in an apartment; in Nanaimo they had an apartment on the waterfront. Cross-Canada flights between Ottawa and The Island were a regular feature as Tommy kept in constant touch with his constituency. It is a dizzying thought to even guess the number of flights Tommy made across Canada during these years.

Tommy's close personal association with his constituents shows in the following stories.

A REAL PREMIER

I have a story to share from my own childhood which I treasure. I can't remember which election it was, but probably 1957 or 1958. I was about six at the time.

Tommy Douglas was the guest speaker at a rally for my grandfather, Colin Cameron, in Nanaimo. My mother and I, and Colin and Dorothy Cameron, my grandmother, had gone to pick up Premier Douglas and Irma. I was very excited at meeting a real premier and the legendary Tommy.

When he got in the car it is family lore that I blurted out, "You can't be a real premier—you're too small and you don't have a top hat." Tommy laughed and laughed and assured me he was real and would come next time with the proper hat.

✍ **Robin V. Sears**

Erhart Regier congratulates Tommy Douglas after his election to the House of Commons in the Burnaby-Coquitlam by-election, October 1962.

THE CHILDREN'S TABLE

The day Tommy was nominated at Chemanius for Nanaimo-Cowichan-The Islands, Dorothy, Colin Cameron's widow and an executive member, had invited everyone to the Cameron home at Lantzville for dinner. There were the people who had nominated Tommy, the chairman of the meeting, and myself, because by now it was assumed that I would be the campaign manager.

In the Cameron house you ate in the kitchen in an area looking over the water. There was also a smaller table for the children. The two tables were set. Tommy hadn't arrived. Finally Mrs. Cameron said, "Well, we will start." So we sat at the dining table overlooking the water.

She had said, "People who come late for dinner get to sit at the children's table." I never thought this would include the Federal Leader of the New Democratic Party, and newly elected candidate. But when the Douglas party arrived, Mrs. Cameron stood up and said, "People who come late for dinner sit at the children's table."

And Tommy promptly sat down.

✍ **Joyce Nash**

A BIT OF A TERROR

From the time he was nominated, Tommy and Irma took up residence in a downtown apartment block in Nanaimo and kept it until the day he gave up representing Nanaimo. Whenever he was in the riding he had a regular route first thing every morning, to walk two blocks to the Malaspina Hotel for his morning bowl of porridge.

Tommy, Jim Manly, Barbara Wallace and Bob Strachan in Duncan, 1979.

As an MP he was sometimes a bit of a terror. He travelled almost without fail every second week back to the riding. When he arrived, he wanted to know what were his commitments for the weekend of two or three days. Unless his time was totally filled, he expressed his displeasure in no uncertain terms by saying, "I didn't come all the way out from Ottawa to sit in my apartment and twiddle my thumbs." There were times when we almost wished he would spend less time in the riding!

Today, some years after Tommy stepped down as MP for Nanaimo-Cowichan-The Islands, I still meet people in my office and in canvassing who remember the personal favours that Tommy was able to do for them.

✍ **Dave Stupich**

TOMMY IN NANAIMO

When Tommy became our candidate I was excited that we would be getting a person of his calibre in Nanaimo-Cowichan-The Islands. I was president of the constituency at the time.

I was excited because of the great work Tommy had done in Saskatchewan.

He was a person who inspired people, inspired people to want to think things out for a better social democracy. He inspired people with his oratory.

I remember talking with Colin Cameron about this; Colin said, "He will always get you laughing but every story has a message."

I remember his ability "to walk with kings and keep the common touch." He had that ability always.

✦ **E. John Cannon**

Irma Douglas, Tommy Douglas and Dorothy Cameron in B.C.

A few years back I hadn't thought so much of Tommy: he couldn't be a Socialist because of some of the things he did. After nine months of travelling with him, I was sure he was as good or a better Socialist as any I ever met.

I think he did appreciate my work.

✿ **Alex McLellan**

TOMMY IS OUR CANDIDATE

We invited Tommy to run in Nanaimo-Cowichan-The Islands following the sudden death of our MP, Colin Cameron. His response was that he would consider it only if he were assured that there was no one locally who wanted the opportunity. He made a point of listening to us and asking people directly whether or not anyone else wanted the nomination. When he was reassured, Tommy became our candidate in the by-election.

One of the highlights of the campaign was when the main highway on the southern approaches to Nanaimo, known as Nicol Street, sprouted so many orange and black Tommy Douglas signs that it was popularly known as "Douglas Street."

✍ **Dave Stupich**

THE CAMPAIGN TRAIL

I can't think of any person that I have heard of in Canada who did as much as Tommy.

I travelled with him for nine months during the by-election here in Nanaimo, practically every day in 1968-1969.

I found him very nice to work with. Things had to be just so, you know. I had so much respect for him. He would have me pick him up at 8:00 in the morning. We would get back maybe at 2:00 or 3:00 the next morning. I would pick him up at 8:00 again the next morning. By that time, he had been in touch with Ottawa, dictating letters and stuff like that. He had been going for a couple of hours before I picked him up.

New Democrats..

Tommy Douglas
Dave Stupich
Ted Miller
working for you year 'round!

Election piece with Tommy Douglas endorsing Dave Stupich and Ted Miller, 1978 federal campaign.

1969 BY-ELECTION

It was the worst winter on the coast. I was in Nanaimo-Cowichan-The Islands for the 1969 by-election. It rained every day and with the rain came snow. Tommy wasn't well but he lived by his guideline that as the candidate you have to work harder—the others are volunteers—you have to work harder than anyone else. We crawled through sawmills in January with the snow and water dripping off everything. He lead that campaign with tenacity and courage.

We set quotas for every poll. Tommy was driving us and working his heart out.

I made appointments to meet all the religious leaders in the city of Duncan in the afternoon. Methodically, Tommy visited each of them: the United Church, the Anglicans, the Evangelical groups, the Roman Catholics.

A young Catholic priest made it a point to criticize "you socialists." After a while, an elderly retired priest, who had been sitting quietly in the background, got up and as he left put his hand on Tommy's shoulder and said, "I was in Saskatchewan at Humboldt and what you did there was a miracle."

We set up a meeting with the Chinese people. Sandy Chung, a woodworker, and his cousin, a businessman, accompanied us as we visited every Chinese household. After being introduced in rapid Chinese and in English, Tommy visited with them, had lunch with them and smoked their tobacco. He won the Chinese vote.

⊛ **Ed Whelan**

Lewie Lloyd and Tommy at a Vancouver rally during 1968 federal campaign.

HE CARRIED HIS OWN SUITCASE

I first met Tommy when he ran in the by-election in Nanaimo-Cowichan-The Islands, 1968-1969.

I was working as business manager for Local 180, International Woodworkers of America, Duncan. I picked him up at the ferry and drove him to Duncan. He was very quiet and businesslike. He carried his own suitcase.

I had read a lot about him. I sensed a great deal of strength in him, a very strong man, a man of conviction. He was humble, he could respond to the average person.

☘ **Hugh Robinson**

A LITTLE SCOTCH AND WATER

We went into a cafe for dinner. Bob and I ordered a beer for our meal, and Tommy ordered wine. That shocked me. I didn't think he drank.

One night at a party at Lake Cowichan we went into what does Tommy drink. The waiter brought our drinks, and said, "What would you like, Mr. Douglas?" "A little Scotch and water."

☘ **Hugh Robinson**

Be My Campaign Manager?

After Colin Cameron died, the decision was made that we would ask Tommy to come here in the by-election we eventually fought in February 1969.

This constituency had withstood the Trudeau sweep. We had the feeling we knew how to win New Democrat campaigns. It had to be someone like Tommy to run in our beloved Colin's seat. It could not be just anyone.

The assumption was that I would be the campaign manager. I said, "No, no," because I believed the campaign manager should be the choice of the candidate, so I said Tommy Douglas would make his choice.

In the meantime I was doing some work for him. One day I got a phone call from Tommy in Vancouver, "My plane is leaving in three hours and I can't find my ticket. Would you search the apartment?" I couldn't find it.

I got back to him and said, "You were wearing your brown Harris tweed jacket when you arrived. Have you got it with you?"

"Yes, in the closet."

So, I said, "Look in the inside pocket," because most men put their tickets in the inside jacket pocket.

So, he went off, then came back and said, "It was in the pocket of my Harris tweed jacket. Would you like to be the campaign manager?"

I have always thought Tommy made his decision about people he wanted to work with him on whether they had horse sense. Instead of saying, "You can go to the airport and they will issue you another ticket," I suggested where to look.

☜ **Joyce Nash**

Tommy Douglas stands on a softdrink case to speak to a rally of 5,000 supporters during the Burnaby-Coquitlam election campaign, 1965.

Tommy Douglas gives victory sign after re-election in Nanaimo-Cowichan-The Islands, 1972.

FIRST IMPRESSION

The first time I met Tommy was going into the elevator in the apartment block in Nanaimo. There were two young teenagers there for whom Tommy had been trying to locate jobs. They were too young to vote. He insisted that they come back and let him know how they made out. I thought to myself they are non-voters, but here is someone who is really concerned about young people, whether they can vote or not. That was my first impression of Tommy, that he was truly concerned for individuals.

✆ Art Morton

A TOUGH CAMPAIGN !

The weather in the 1969 campaign was terrible, ice and snow, lots of accidents. I broke my ankle on the farm. It was a very bad break. I was on crutches. My car was an automatic so I could drive. The day before the election we had meetings of workers, to get our kits.

As I drove up, coming across the parkade was a fellow who obviously had broken his collar bone. His arm was at right angles up in the air. Tommy was at the door greeting all the workers. He took a look at us. He shook his head and said, "Well, I knew it had been a tough campaign but I didn't know it had been that tough!"

✆ Barbara Wallace

CLOSE ENCOUNTER

Tommy was an orator. He had a golden tongue. But there was more to it than that. He was a worker, an indefatigable worker. He wore us all out. I will always remember my first really close introduction to Tommy. We got the election committee set up. Tommy arrived from Ottawa and we had a meeting in somebody's house. He came in with his charming, affable greetings. Then Tommy said, "What have you been doing? Have you got signs?" Well, no, we didn't have any signs. "Have you got anybody canvassing?" Well, no, we didn't have anybody canvassing. "Well, have you got committee rooms?" Well, no, we didn't have committee rooms. "What have you been doing all this time? We have to get this thing going." He blew his top at all of us. We then started to get going.

    ☉ **Barbara Wallace**

Barbara Wallace with Tommy Douglas, 1980.

KEEP THE TROOPS TOGETHER

The 1972 campaign was difficult here because we'd just had a provincial election. I think we had 12 days going into the federal campaign. I remember Tommy phoning from Ottawa and saying, "Keep the troops together. I think we're going to go," and my saying, "No, the troops are going down even if they only have a few days. They have got to go home." He wanted to keep them on election readiness, and he had been part of the provincial campaign as well.

    ☉ **Joyce Nash**

HARD TO WORK FOR?

I remember having a discussion with Tommy after the 1969 provincial campaign here, which in my opinion had not been a very good campaign for the New Democrats. It had not been tight and our leader missed press conferences and arrived late for meetings. I tended to blame a lot of it on staff, Mr. X.

I said to Tommy, "Mr. X wouldn't last two days working for you." There was a pause, then Tommy looked at me and said, "Joyce, do you think I am hard to work for?" Tommy wasn't, in my opinion, hard to work for, but he was difficult for some people. But I thought that he really hadn't any idea that he was hard to work for.

    ☉ **Joyce Nash**

THE PRACTICAL POLITICIAN

Yes, Tommy was a caring and dedicated man but he was also a very practical one. Along with his vision of the future, and his ability to translate that vision into spellbinding words, Tommy Douglas recognized the importance of facing up to the day-to-day challenges.

I recall a meeting of the Cowichan Malahat NDP Constituency Association convened about a month after the 1975 December election. The NDP government had gone down to defeat and the premier, Dave Barrett, had lost his seat. It was, also, my first campaign as the candidate. We had managed to hang on to the seat held for so long by my predecessor, Bob Strachan.

It had been agreed by the party and caucus that Barrett should seek election in a riding other than where he had been defeated. A certain amount of polling had been undertaken to test the water in various constituencies, including Cowichan Malahat. The rumour was out that I might be stepping down after only one month as MLA, so you can understand why the hall was fairly well packed for the meeting. Tommy was in attendance as our Member of Parliament in Ottawa.

There was a fairly lengthy discussion on the pros and cons of having a by-election and on the prospect of Dave Barrett as our MLA. In the end the decision was left to me. (I did not step down; I sat in the B.C. Legislature until 1986.)

Tommy Douglas on the hustings in B.C., 1968.

After the meeting Tommy took me aside and gave me two pieces of advice.

The first went something like this: "Don't underestimate your own ability. You are just as able as anyone else."

The second came almost as an afterthought: "Go to the bathroom whenever you have an opportunity,- it may be a long time before you get another chance!"

Through the years I came to recognize the value of following both suggestions.

⚶ Barbara Wallace

Cliff Scotton, Joyce Nash (campaign manager), Robin Sears, Tommy Douglas (candidate), Mary Smith, Irma Douglas, Alex McLellan, and Rita Glen on election night when Tommy was elected MP for Nanaimo-Cowichan-The Islands, February 1969.

MEETING YOUNG PEOPLE

Tommy had a very busy itinerary. If we didn't have something lined up for him every five minutes, he thought he wasn't fulfilling his job. This particular day he had a meeting in the afternoon, a dinner meeting, and for the evening a little party for the young people.

I got everything set up at the apartment and was there before anyone came. They were supposed to be there at 7:30 pm. Tommy came in at 7:25 and said, "I just have to change." He was wearing a suit and tie. He dashed into the bedroom. The kids started to come, and Tommy came out. He had taken off his shirt, tie and jacket and put on a turtle-neck. He had kicked off his shoes and put on slippers. There he was lounging around with the kids; all in five minutes, a different person from the man who came in at 7:25, all business-like and professional.

⊕ **Barbara Wallace**

Tommy and Irma Douglas phone Tommy's mother in Winnipeg to let her know he had been elected in Burnaby-Coquitlam, 1965.

TOUGHMINDED TOMMY

I remember Tommy when I was the publicity committee chairperson for Ted Miller's election campaign, how very political and toughminded Douglas was. Nobody who watched Tommy at close quarters could ever confuse him with being wimpish or bleeding heart in his approach.

In our discussions about budgets and whether we could afford to do all the things that we ought to do, given our limited resources, Douglas' comments were very clear—and I can even quote them: "Spend the money and buy the signs. We'll find the money after."

I also witnessed Tommy in campaign headquarters when he observed that things were not being done quite as they should. That gentle and kind and altogether charming man, who would never say anything to hurt or offend or perplex the average campaign worker, could be very brusque and blunt with people who were supposed to be capable and who had accordingly been given greater responsibility.

He once told a sign chairman—in no uncertain terms, that the pile of signs sitting in the corner of the committee rooms was not doing us much good, and that the sign chairman would do well to get outside the building and put up the signs, rather than stay in the office and pretend to look busy and official.

✍ **Dale Lovick**

NO SITTING AROUND

In an election campaign, particularly towards the end, he seemed to be almost hyper. If anyone was sitting around he wanted them out there pounding the pavement.

We had a bunch of canvassers come over from Vancouver. We teamed them up with local people who didn't know anything about canvassing but knew the district. There was one guy left over and there was a chap sitting in the office, so I grabbed him. "Here, you know this district. You go out with him." Away they went. It turned out the guy from Vancouver was waiting for his wife. But I knew Tommy expected everyone in the committee room to work.

✆ **Art Morton**

Dave Stupich, David Lewis, Irma Douglas, Tommy Douglas, and Bob Strachan, South Burnaby high school, NDP provincial convention, 1968.

LETTER TO TREASURE

When Dave Barrett stepped down as leader of the New Democrats in British Columbia in June of 1983, I made a decision to run for that position. I thought that Tommy might prefer not to get involved in that kind of contest, but one of my friends did write to him asking whether or not he would give me a letter of endorsement. He responded promptly and so positively that I was almost embarrassed to use the letter. It is one of the treasures in my personal archives.

✍ **Dave Stupich**

Dave Barrett, Allan Blakeney and Tommy Douglas at a federal pre-convention political education conference in Vancouver, 1974.

USELESS EXERCISE

My first memory of Tommy was when he attended an executive meeting of the B.C. New Democrats. I think it was in 1970 while I was serving as provincial president. Tommy happened to be in town, knew about the executive meeting and wandered in. We were discussing the sort of things that executives do discuss to no particular long-range benefit and then got to election planning.

Tommy listened for a while and then spoke up:

"How many votes did the New Democrats get in the 1969 provincial election? How many members does the party have in B.C. today?"

When he was given the answers, he responded:

"For you people to be sitting around here talking about winning the next election when you have substantially less than 10% of your supporters signed up as members is about as useless an exercise as anyone can imagine."

I took his message to heart and, together with the provincial secretary, made sure that we signed up enough members to exceed our 10% target.

✍ **Dave Stupich**

◆ 6 ◆

Retired Statesman ◆ 1979-1986

Tommy retired from active politics in 1979. Perhaps the correspondence lessened but Tommy and Eleanor McKinnon—his secretary since 1944—continued to answer letters from across Canada and around the world. They worked out of the office of the Douglas-Coldwell Foundation. Tommy promoted the Foundation's aims: research, publication and discussion in the pursuit of socialist ideas and ideals for a better Canada in a better world.

Tommy accepted many invitations to speak. His addresses contained a timeless message: "Never be afraid of something just because it is new. . . . Never discard something just because it is old. . . . Measure your life, not by what you get but by what you give."

Today's leaders tell us what they learned from Tommy. Many men and women at the local level were also encouraged by Tommy, he kept in touch with them, inspired them, and challenged them to go forward.

He demonstrated that the busiest person can take on additional or new responsibility. In spite of failing health, masked by self-control and his smile, he travelled and spoke to meetings and to individuals—and always, with hope and humour.

A Grandson Speaks

"Jesse Jackson was telling this terrible story about a poor black woman who had arrived at the hospital hemorrhaging to death and how they wouldn't deliver her baby because she had no money," Sutherland recalls.

Another Canadian in the group said such a thing would never happen in Canada because of national medicare. At which point Sutherland piped up to his assembled friends: "Yes and it was my grandfather who started it."

It gave the 21-year-old Sutherland enormous pride to make that comment, to pay homage to the man who was perhaps the greatest single influence on him when he was growing up; his grandfather, Tommy Douglas.

Virtually no one in Los Angeles knows that Kiefer is the grandson of the most successful socialist politician in North America's history—the man who headed Saskatchewan's CCF government for 18 years, and laid the groundwork for the introduction of medicare in that province before taking on the national leadership of the CCF's successor, the New Democratic Party.

The bedrock of Sutherland's beliefs is the memory of his grandfather, who instilled in him a concern for human right and dignity.

"I knew my grandfather real well. He did raise me a lot and he was a real influence."

The first book Tommy Douglas ever gave his grandson was a biography of Clarence Darrow, the legendary U.S. lawyer and civil rights advocate.

"I'll never forget reading it for the first time, because for me it revealed the ideals my grandfather believed in. Morally, politically, socially—at all levels he basically set out my

Kiefer Sutherland, grandson of Tommy Douglas, four years old.

moral values system for me.

"My grandfather was the one who encouraged me to act. I remember saying to him, 'I feel really weird about this because my mom does it and my dad does it.' And he said, 'You just go and do your thing and you'll be fine.'

"I guess you could say that my grandfather instilled beliefs in me and also a great deal of faith in myself. He really made me feel I was something." Kiefer pauses, and then adds, "Of course, he made a lot of people feel that way, didn't he?"

✄ **Kiefer Sutherland**
interviewed by Jamie Portman

Tommy Douglas; Reg Basken, president of the Alberta Federation of Labour; and Grant Notley, leader of the Alberta NDP, at a rally in Edmonton, 1975.

GRANT WANTED TOMMY

I was working as an organizer in the 1982 campaign in Alberta. Canvass results were not what we would have liked. We were not doing well at all. Tommy Douglas was not feeling well and could not commit himself to a rally for Grant Notley. Allan Blakeney came to a rally in the south part of the constituency, but still Grant wanted Tommy.

Tommy had been in Grant's constituency in all other campaigns—1971, 1975, 1979. Without Tommy in 1982, Grant thought his political success might suffer. There were more phone calls and finally—the last Sunday before E-day—we got Tommy. One could see that he was tired yet he took the stage and delivered a speech that brought tears to the eyes of many when he talked about the goals and dreams of the Party.

Following the rally, he came back to the committee rooms to encourage all the workers. At some point in the day I was driving him about town and thanked him for coming. His response was something to the effect that, "Grant had struggled alone for so long that it was the least I could do."

✍ **Tom Sigurdson**

Tommy Douglas autographing copies of J.S. Woodsworth's "Grace Before Meals" during a visit to Weyburn.

HOW'S THE BUS?

In Tommy's last days of retirement in Ottawa he used to walk out on the driveway. He had forgotten that on the weekend the bus service was given the right-of-way in what was normally a one-way street. The result was that Tommy was run into and landed in hospital. He was ill at the time already and we thought, this is terrible, this is going to destroy him totally. A few days later he bounded back. Everyone around Ottawa was saying, "Oh, Tommy's all right, but how's the bus!"

✦ **Walter B. Mann**

BUILDING A NEW SOCIETY

There was a basic sincerity and conviction that always came through from Tommy Douglas. When you talked to him and when he talked about meeting the needs of people, you knew he meant it. He wasn't just looking for votes. He honestly wanted to build a new society and he believed that we had the power to do it.

They talk today about politicians and charisma. I happen to think that Douglas had it, as a gift, it wasn't contrived, it wasn't something he tried to develop. It was just there.

And the reason it was there was that he saw himself as having a mission and he would work toward that end.

✦ **Alex Taylor**

AFTER THE MEETING

My mother-in-law, Miriam Larmour, had been an avid Tommy Douglas supporter since the 1930s. One morning in 1980, he was to be in Lanigan addressing a meeting. She was brokenhearted, for she was in the hospital and could not attend.

After the meeting, someone told Tommy that Mrs. Larmour, a long-time supporter, had been so upset because she could not come to shake his hand. He asked where she was and went to visit her. Before he left, he kissed my dear 80-year-old, ninety pound mother-in-law on the cheek.

This quiet, soft spoken lady, her eyes shining, said, "I'm not going to wash that cheek, ever."

✎ **Jean Larmour**

TOMMY AT RATCLIFFE

Tommy made his first political speech in a little town called Ratcliffe on behalf of my uncle Eric Oxelgren. Uncle Eric ran in Bromhead and Tommy Douglas ran in the Weyburn seat in the 1934 provincial election.

Many years later, Tommy made his last political speech in Ratcliffe. It was about 1983, we went down to supper at the Co-op hall. A great crowd of folks gathered there, including some who had been at the first meeting.

They recalled the first meeting. It had rained at Ratcliffe. There were no paved roads, no gravel roads. Tommy rolled up his pant legs and took off his shoes in order to help push the car to get it into Ratcliffe.

There were about 180 folks at the banquet in 1983. Tommy was in extra good form. He reminded people about the many good things that began at that first meeting in Ratcliffe.

I was the only person travelling to Regina, so my youngest daughter and I had the good luck to be able to take Tommy home. It was a terrific experience for us to talk with Tommy for the two and a half hour trip to Regina.

As I recall the trip, I talked about half the time to Tommy, Tommy talked all the time, and Lisa would talk with him when I wasn't talking with him. Lisa was 16 at the time. It

MP Grace MacInnis (nee Woodsworth) and Tommy Douglas at the House of Commons, January 1971. Grace met Tommy in Winnipeg in 1934 at a CCYM convention. She was Caucus secretary when he was elected MP in 1935, and later served as both an MLA and MP from B.C.

has left an impression on Lisa and caused her to be interested in political science.

Lisa thought it was just the greatest and she has referred to it several times since. It was almost like being with a prophet.

Tommy impressed on her to get the most she could out of education, and to do some public service for her country.

☸ **Stan Oxelgren**

AFTER GRANT DIED

One week after Grant Notley's death I was invited to a Federal Council meeting to do a tribute to Grant. One of the first people I saw was Tommy Douglas. I can remember how upset he was—tears and everything—a very human man.

The Monday morning after our Provincial Convention which acclaimed me leader, the first phone call I received was from Tommy Douglas congratulating and encouraging me. I will always remember that thoughtfulness in what was a tough time for me and the Alberta NDP.

✍ **Ray Martin**

Irma and Tommy Douglas with Doreen and Alvin Hewitt, part of the group that visited Weyburn following the 50th Anniversary convention in Regina, July 1983.

A PRAIRIE MAN

. . . He was a prairie man, nurtured by our winds.
His laughing eyes were touched by prairie skies.
Prairie stars reached down, graced the soul within.
As sons of prairie dust, we will remember him.

✂ **D. S. Curry**

TOMMY REMEMBERS EMMETT

My husband, Emmett Johnson, was active in the CCF/NDP from 1935 until his death in 1979. In May 1977 he was in hospital in Saskatoon when Tommy came to speak in the Centennial Auditorium. Emmett was able to get hospital leave to attend the meeting. So, wheelchair and all, we set out. We used the service elevator and his chair was placed at the end of a row in the aisle.

Tommy came marching in behind the bagpipes. He saw Emmett and came right over to shake his hand. "Emmett, what are you doing in that thing? What happened?" Tommy spent a few minutes talking to Emmett, then was on his way up the aisle.

✍ **Betty Johnson**

David Lewis, Sophie Lewis, Shirley Carr and Irma and Tommy Douglas on the platform at the 1980 CLC convention in Winnipeg. David Lewis and Tommy Douglas were both presented with awards for outstanding service to humanity.

MID-CENTURY COLOSSUS

The great keening mystery of every life is to figure out the existential why. The context in which people shape who they are is difficult enough to see clearly, but the content of a person is such a chimera that few can see their own definition. The meaning of existence tends, on an individual basis, to be more or less illusive. It is a puzzle, therefore, that Tommy Douglas acquired serene certainty of what he was about.

The era in which he strode Canadian politics like a colossus was mid-century, a time of the Great Depression, the Second World War and a euphoric recovery. Problems then were no less complex and insoluble than they are now, but Tommy Douglas never found them so. He always believed that people were better than they knew and that whatever was unjust in society could be fixed.

✂ **June Callwood**

AIRPORT SERVICE

On one occasion, shortly after I was elected Leader of the Manitoba New Democratic Party in 1980, I attended a banquet in Brandon. Tommy was guest speaker. After the banquet the Brandon people asked me if I would drive Tommy back to the Winnipeg airport.

I was delighted because it was an opportunity for me, as recently elected Leader of the Opposition, to gain some insight from Tommy's experience. Adele, my wife, was with me. That three-hour drive went by like 20 minutes because it was such a moving, invigorating and intellectually satisfying experience.

Tommy gave me some advice that I was able to follow successfully afterwards.

First, he emphasized over and over the importance of focusing, and I think to this day that a lot of our political people do not focus properly. Tommy said you check out the weak spot in the party opposing you and you pounce upon it and you keep hitting away at it. At that time in Manitoba the economy was in difficult straits under Lyon and as a result we concentrated on an attack on the economy; job loss, sons and daughters leaving the province in record numbers. We concentrated on that.

He said, form task forces for Caucus to go round the province. Have a task force on social issues, one on agriculture, one on the economy. We formed task forces and we had task forces going all over the province for the next two years. We formed these task forces, but it was Tommy's idea that he shared with me on that trip from Brandon to Winnipeg. I think it was one of the best things we did; it may have contributed in a very large way to our election in November 1981 because the task forces were extremely successful. We had a lot of harmony within our caucus. Everyone pulled together and it worked out very well.

Tommy Douglas and Stanley Knowles at a Retirement Evening for Stanley Knowles in Winnipeg, November 3, 1983.

I should just mention that when we got to the airport in Winnipeg, Tommy ran into the airport. We didn't have much time, I think we were just within minutes. To my surprise every counter clerk recognized Tommy. I guess I shouldn't have been surprised. They treated him as though he was a friend—here in Winnipeg, not Regina or Saskatoon, and they were calling, "Tommy, Tommy."

✈ **Howard Pawley**

WATCHING TOMMY

A child's mind collects images. Often the meaning of what we see as children is only clear years later. Watching Tommy through childhood leaves many pictures.

Tommy on the mound with the pitcher at a CCF picnic, playing ump before the pitch is complete. The crowd howling with laughter.

Tommy climbing out of his car during a parade to walk the route and talk to people along the way. This happened regularly and often a group of children would end up walking the route with him.

Tommy encouraging young people in the audience to go to a mike and ask their questions. Waiting until they are at the mike.

Tommy tolerating the most abrasive heckling this writer has heard, then or since. Treating everyone who heckled with patience and humour. Often directing the audience to not intercede.

Tommy telling stories, where the room would go from absolute silence to total laughter in seconds. Those stories working over and over again. And the people telling them. As a child the fun was when I'd overhear one of Tommy's stories on the playground.

Tommy doing what we now call 'working the room'. He would speak to everyone twice. Once when they arrived and went through the receiving line and then when he moved from table to table. No one was left out, including those who wanted to complain.

Tommy being marched in with the bagpipes. Rallies, conventions, meetings all started that way. Always joyous, always stops along the way to the platform, and always a joke first. Often he would lead the singing of CCF songs of solidarity.

The images of Tommy among people, at picnics, parades, touring the exhibition, on the grounds of the Legislature, in the hall at conventions, at teas, after meetings when hundreds would stay to talk to him—these are the strongest. There are no images of turning away from anyone.

The images of passion, anger, and conviction are there. They did not affect me as a child. Years later they meant that this man worked, fought, was committed and never stopped trying to improve the quality of life for Canadians.

✍ **Gaile Whelan-Enns**

THE WEYBURN CO-OP

Tommy was guest speaker in 1979 when we celebrated the 50th anniversary of the Weyburn Co-op. The Co-op began in 1929, the year before Tommy came to Weyburn.

During the 1940s, the Co-op rented part of the McKinnon Building, a three-storey structure, down town. And in 1950 the Co-op bought the building. With Tommy's help. He came along one day and said, "You know, the Co-op should buy this building. I think the McKinnons would sell it."

He got in touch with Keith McKinnon in Toronto, and talked to the board and the Co-op purchased the McKinnon Building for $87,500. We mortgaged for another $5,000, making the mortgage $92,500 which was paid off in two or three years.

Tommy's help with the negotiations was just an indication of how interested he continued to be in this community.

⚙ **Isabelle Butters**

Tommy Douglas; Dennis McDermott, president of the CLC; and Ed Broadbent at the NDP federal convention, 1983.

TOMMY VISITED MY GREAT-GRANDMOTHER

I met Tommy twice. The second occasion was in Regina in 1983 when he gave that unforgettable speech at the 50th anniversary.

The first time was in the late 1950s in Yorkton. I was a youngster with a paper route. My great-grandmother Kehoe was being cared for in a private home which happened to be on my route. Tommy came to see her, I met him and I was so impressed that the Premier would come to visit my elderly great-grandmother.

⚙ **Brian Pitchford**

BASIC VALUES

As leader I am struggling with getting a philosophy that is relevant to the ordinary people, finding a political voice. I'm doing a lot of reading, including Tommy's speeches and books about Tommy. I'm finding that speaking to values, basic values—freedom and independence and people working together—becomes the touchstone upon which I am basing my actions.

That Tommy's words are still being espoused by the leadership of today indicates the depth and soundness of his philosophy.

⚙ **Roy Romanow**

Gordon Snyder and Tommy at the opening of the T.C. Douglas Building, Regina, 1979.

SHARED MEMORIES

In 1979, I had the rare good fortune, as Saskatchewan's Minister of Government Services, to preside over the ceremony when our new provincial Health Building was officially opened in Regina, and named the T.C. Douglas Building.

It remains as a permanent and fitting monument to the man and his ideals.

People from all parts of the province and beyond came to honour Tommy, and to stay for several hours after the official program to clasp his hand, recalling stories of days gone by.

Tommy stayed as long as there was a visitor who wanted to shake his hand. Those who clasped his hand and shared memories with him returned to their homes remembering the warmth, the charm and the true Christian ideals which caused me, as a young man, to venture to play a part in Tommy's vision of a more just and humane social democratic community.

✍ **Gordon T. Snyder**

TOMMY'S CANE

Ed and I were in Eastern Canada in August 1985. Before going to Ottawa, we had been in touch with Tommy and Irma and had been invited to visit them.

Getting out of the airport bus at the hotel, I fell, spraining an ankle. It became very painful, so we phoned Irma to explain what had happened. She said that after Tommy's nap they would come to the hotel to see us. (He was very ill but seemed his usual positive, friendly self.) As they came in the door, Tommy handed me a cane saying, "Perhaps you can use this."

The grandchildren admire the slim ebony cane with its gold knob and ferrule. They'd like to handle it. Although I belong to what Ed calls the give-them-the-clock-and-a-hammer school of grandmothers, Tommy's cane is not a plaything. "A very great man, Tommy Douglas, gave me this cane," I explain, "so we won't play with it."

A cane, support for a sprained ankle, is a reminder to me of Tommy's thoughtfulness; in the larger sense it also reminds us of the support so many others in Saskatchewan received from Tommy when they needed it.

✍ **Pemrose Whelan**

TOMMY MADE HISTORY HAPPEN

I wager that coming generations will count Tommy Douglas among the wise—a man ahead of his time who made a better history happen.

✂ **Grant Maxwell**

Tommy Douglas Speaks

When I approached Tommy about doing my book, I had given no thought whatsoever to making any money from the endeavour and, therefore, when Tommy asked what we proposed to do about royalties I said that I didn't expect to get anything.

He looked at me with that rather quizzical and somewhat perplexed furrowing of the brow characteristic of him—which also suggested that my naivety was evident — and told me that I had better get something for my labours. He went on to suggest that if I wanted to be generous I could donate some part of the royalties to the Douglas-Coldwell Foundation.

I didn't spend more than about one hour in total talking to Tommy about the book. Part of the reason was that I wanted to be the "objective" academic—despite my New Democratic Party membership and my obvious sympathies—and therefore wanted to let Douglas' recorded words tell the story by themselves.

John Larter. Reprinted with permission - The Toronto Star Syndicate.

I felt reluctant to ask for any of his time and therefore did not do so. The point, though, is that he was prepared to help me and told his former executive assistant, Richard McLellan, to give me whatever I wanted and to answer any questions. Tommy was prepared to get me anything I needed in putting the book together.

✍ **Dale Lovick**

Irma Douglas, Tommy Douglas, Auburn Pepper and George Hoffman at Tommy Douglas Night in Weyburn, 1980.

LOOKING UP TO TOMMY

Tommy was an example that people looked up to. I don't think people regarded him as a politician, they regarded him as a leader who had conviction and integrity. They admired him for his personality and for the visionary aspects of his thinking.

        George R. Bothwell

TOMMY'S 1983 SPEECH

The greatest memory I have of Tommy was his last major speech when he addressed the 1983 federal convention of the New Democrats in Regina. I believe he knew he was suffering a terminal illness. He was very tired.

He spoke for an hour and it was the kind of message that the Party needed at that time. I have never heard or experienced anything like it. When he was finished he must have been totally exhausted although it didn't show. However, those near him knew. They tried to usher him off the platform but the assembly, realizing that it would probably be his last major effort and recognizing the importance of the speech itself, insisted with standing ovations on calling him back time after time.

        Dave Stupich

Tommy Douglas greets Goldie Thair in the Regina North West committee rooms during the 1978 Saskatchewan election campaign.

Douglas As MP

. . . But on the platform he appeared neither as a revolutionary nor a politician. He looked rather like the president of a small-town Rotary Club—a slight and dapper little man, five feet five inches in height, 140 pounds in weight, with the keen face of a terrier and a tongue which framed wisecracks too easily. His speeches had a firecracker quality to them, exploding in all directions, but hardly shattering the foundations of Canada. With the sure instincts of the showman he mixed his social protest with funny stories of the more obvious sort and the people found him earnest but amusing.

He fought as he had fought in the amateur boxing ring in Manitoba, where he held the amateur light-weight championship— fought with sudden, quick punches, rapid footwork and, above all, with courage. He did not make himself popular in Parliament but he made himself heard and, at times, he could penetrate even the rhinoceros skin of the Government.

✄ **Bruce Hutchison**

Tommy Douglas in Ottawa in 1983. The House of Commons can be seen in the background.

Speech Of His Life

Probably the greatest speech in his life was in 1983 in Regina at the 50th annual convention. The greatness of the thing, with everyone else floundering in uncertainty, it was a very simple speech, nothing complicated. Some very simple ideas, not too many of them to digest.

Ⓐ **T.H. (Tommy) McLeod**

APPENDIX

CONTRIBUTORS

When the province is not given, read **Saskatchewan.** Names starred (*) are those who helped in a variety of ways including unpublished anecdotes.

Alexander, Hugh of Weyburn. Retired farmer. Weyburn Co-op member No. 6. Wheat Pool member since 1935. Former Weyburn constituency CCF president.

Anderson, Eldon of Regina. Grew up on father's homestead in the Cadillac/Val Marie district. Worked as information officer and editor with the CCF government, and for many years for credit unions and co-ops including international co-ops. Active in anti-poverty groups.

Anderson, Jean of Regina. Born in Lang. Registered nurse.

Archer, John H. of Regina. Born in Pipestone Valley of southeast Sask. Authority on Saskatchewan history on radio and TV, in print and as guest speaker. Former Principal and later, President, University of Regina. Author of *Saskatchewan, A History* (Western Producer Prairie Books, 1980).

Arnason, B.N. (Barney) of Vancouver, B.C. Born in Iceland, grew up on farm at Gladstone, Man. Former Registrar and Deputy Minister, Saskatchewan Department of Co-operatives and Co-operative Development. Active as well in national and international co-ops. Spent five years with Canadian International Development Agency in Zambia.

*Baker, Jack & Betty of Nanaimo, B.C.

Banda, Tom & Mary of Regina. Natives of Kayville. Long-time Regina residents and key members of the Romanian Canadian Cultural Club.

Barrett, Pam of Edmonton, Alta. Native of Brandon, Man. Graduate of Universities of Alberta and Glasgow. Researcher for late Grant Notley, Leader, Alberta NDP. NDP MLA elected in 1986, re-elected in 1989, Official Opposition House Leader, Alberta Legislature.

*Beech, Harvey & Peggy of Victoria, B.C.

Beggs, Sam of Weyburn. Retired. Head gardener, Saskatchewan Hospital, Weyburn, 27 years. Horticulture judge for 50 years. Alderman for 14 years. Active in CCF since 1930s.

Benjamin, Les of Regina. Born in Medicine Hat, Alta. CPR station agent for 15 years. Provincial Secretary, Saskatchewan CCF/NDP for seven years. MP since 1968.

Bethel, Eva of Weyburn. Born on father's homestead near Ralph.

Bix, Marvin (born in Rapid City, Iowa) and **Dorothy nee Cripps** (born in Estevan) of McAllen, Texas. Retired. Frequent visitors to Saskatchewan to see Dorothy's relatives and because of their interest in the CCF.

Blakeney, Allan E. Born in Bridgewater, N.S. Rhodes Scholar. Law graduate from Dalhousie. To Saskatchewan in 1950, legal advisor to Government Finance Office. Regina CCF/NDP MLA, 1960-1987, former cabinet minister, Premier of Saskatchewan, Leader of the Opposition.

Borrowman, Roy of Ganges, Salt Spring Island, B.C. Raised in Weyburn district. Former teacher; Executive Secretary, Co-operative Union of Saskatchewan; CCF government public servant for 28 years.

Bothwell, George R. of Regina. Born in Winnipeg, Man. Grew up in Regina. Recalls the Regina Riot, July 1, 1935. Former journalist, advertising and public relations firm; Regina alderman; CCF/NDP candidate. Member, Regina Public Library Board 26 years, chairman since 1986; active in library associations and Heritage groups.

Boyle, Lorraine (nee Butters) of Weyburn.

Broadbent, Ed. Born in Oshawa, Ont. Taught high school English and political science at York University. Ph.D. from London School of Economics. Vice-president Socialist International, 1978-1989. NDP MP, 1968-1989. Federal NDP Leader, 1975-1989.

Brock, Brandon (Bud) of Weyburn. Retired farmer. Former Wheat Pool committee member, United Church secretary, RM councillor.

Brockelbank, John E. of Saskatoon. Born at Tisdale. Instrument technician. NDP MLA since 1964, former cabinet minister and Speaker of the House.

Brown, Percy of Victoria, B.C. Born at Lebret. Worked as railway employee out of Melville; photographer. Former welterweight champion; CCF MLA, 1952-1956; Saskatchewan CCF Provincial Secretary.

Bruce, Charles (Chuck) of Weyburn. Born at Grand Coulee. Grew up at Kronau. Served with RCAF. Technician with Saskatchewan Hospital, Weyburn, for 35 years.

Butters, Isabelle of Weyburn. Born near Weyburn. Weyburn Co-op employee since 1945, General Manager since 1978. Alderman 12 years, mayor six years, Board member: library, Grace United Church, special care home.

Cannon, E. John of Nanaimo, B.C. Born in Vancouver. Army service. Long-time mill engineer; active in union. Former member, Cowichan (urban) Council.

*Cherniack, Saul & Sybil of Winnipeg, Man.

Clements, Gareld K. of Wilcox.

Coleman, Roy of Weyburn. Born in Weyburn. Logged in Northern Saskatchewan in 1930s. Overseas, in Italy four years, World War II. Retired farmer.

Comber, Richard of Toronto, Ont. Born in Montreal. Former vice-president, Quebec NDP, and federal NDP executive member; frequent campaign manager, including in Saskatoon. Life insurance broker.

Cooper Hunt, Marjorie (1901-1984). Born in Manitoba; Regina resident from 1907. Teacher; active in Regina Council of Women (life member), United Church, Regina YWCA. Regina CCF/NDP MLA, 1952-1967.

Cottrill, M.E. of Wynyard.

Cugnet, R.A. of Weyburn. Born near Ralph. Worked in Peace River, U.S. and B.C. in 1930s. After Army service, returned to family farm.

Davidson, Helen of Weyburn. Born in Morganston, Ont., moved to Winnipeg as small child, then to Weyburn. Met Tommy Douglas at Brandon College. Music teacher, taught Shirley Douglas. Baptist Church organist 1930-1987.

Davies, W.G. (Bill) of Regina. Born in Indian Head, grew up in Regina. Worked for Swift Canadian Co., Moose Jaw. Former Moose Jaw alderman; executive secretary, Saskatchewan Federation of Labour for 28 years. CCF/NDP MLA, 1956-1971, and cabinet minister.

Dean, Merril of Yellowknife, NWT. She was born in Saskatoon, grew up in North Battleford. Travelled in People's Republic of China. Teacher, political organizer. Recent Director of Communications, Saskatchewan NDP, and *Commonwealth* editor.

Delahoy, Chris & Jeanne of Cut Knife. Chris was long-time Saskatchewan Wheat Pool employee.

Dodds, W. Earl of Prince Albert.

*Dorey, Iva E. of Weyburn.

*Douglas, Irma of Ottawa, Ont.

Durant, Peggy of Saskatoon.

Durst, Leroy W. of Oungre. Born in Estevan. Air Force service. Wheat Pool committee member for 27 years. Saskatchewan Farmers' Union member 25 years. Long-time CCF/NDP provincial and federal executive member.

Eddy Brock, Veronica of McTaggart. Born near Hoffer. Her book, *The Valley of Flowers* (Coteau Books, Moose Jaw, 1988), reflects her five-year stay at Fort San.

Eliason, Magnus of Winnipeg, Man. Born in Arnes, Man. Homesteaded in Peace River. Long-time CCF/NDP organizer, began in 1932 in Vancouver. Former Winnipeg alderman.

Fines, Clarence M. of Ft. Lauderdale, Fla. Born in Darlingford, Man. To Saskatchewan in 1923. Former teacher; Regina alderman; founding member of Regina Independent Labour Party and Saskatchewan ILP, Farmer-Labour Party, and CCF; Regina CCF MLA, Provincial Treasurer and Deputy Premier, 1944-1960.

Fines, Murray of Regina.

Finn, Ed of Ottawa, Ont. Born in Spaniard's Bay, Nfld. First Newfoundland CCF/NDP leader; candidate. Printer, journalist, editor. Senior public relations officer, Canadian Union of Public Employees.

Fox, Christena & *Joe of Weyburn.

Goranson, Don of Weyburn. Farmer. RCAF service. Member, Flying Farmers.

*Goranson, Doug & Mayvis of Weyburn.

Gorski, Fr. Isidore of Regina. Born on farm near Odessa. Attended University of Toronto; graduate work in Rome; lecturer, University of Regina—helped establish religious studies as degree program. Former chairman, Appeals Committee, Highway Traffic Board. Since 1987 Dean of Campion College, University of Regina.

Harcourt, Mike of Victoria, B.C. Born in Edmonton; grew up in Vancouver. Lawyer. Storefront legal services program, first in Canada, forerunner of legal aid clinics. Vancouver alderman, 1972-1980, mayor, 1980-1986. NDP MLA since 1986, leader B.C. NDP since 1987.

Hatch, Mrs. Wilma of Oak Lake, Man.

Hewitt, Alvin of Perdue. Born in Saskatoon. Father was a 1905 homesteader. Registered Select Seed Grower 30 years. CCF/NDP provincial executive member 15 years, six years as president; federal executive member 12 years, four years as president. Chairman, CCF 50th anniversary convention, Regina 1983.

*Hoffman, George of Weyburn.

Johnson, Beth (Mrs. Barney) of Saskatoon. Born in South Dakota, lived in Wynyard district for many years, then Regina.

Johnson, Betty (Mrs. Emmett) of Spiritwood.

King, Carlyle (1907-1988). Born in Cooksville, Ont. Joined University of Saskatchewan English department in 1929, retired as Dean of Academic Services in 1977. Edited *Saskatchewan Harvest* for Saskatchewan's Golden Jubilee (McClelland & Stewart, 1955). President of Saskatchewan CCF, 1945-1960.

Kowalchuk, John R. of Melville. Born near Goodeve. Former teacher, reeve, school board chairman; Wheat Pool committee, Co-op and Credit Union member; NDP MLA, 1967-1982, and cabinet minister.

Kramer, Eiling of North Battleford. Born near North Battleford. Rancher, auctioneer. Former Saskatchewan Farmers' Union vice-president; CCF/NDP MLA, 1952-1980; cabinet minister; "Dean of House."

Larmour, Jean B.D. of Regina. Born Jean Shepley in North Battleford. Former sessional instructor, University of Regina. Senior researcher for *Saskatchewan, A History* by John H. Archer. Author of *University Women's Club of Regina* (1985), *A Matter of Life and Breath* (1989).

Lee, H.S. (Tim) of Toronto, Ont. Born at Galt, Ont. To Saskatchewan in 1948, economic advisor to Advisory and Planning Board; executive assistant to Premier and cabinet secretary. Now teaches at U. of T.

Lindsay, Mrs. Hildred of Winnipeg, Man.

Little, Mrs. Elizabeth of Assiniboia.

Lloyd, Woodrow S. (1913-1972). Born to pioneer parents on farm northwest of Webb. Principal of Biggar school when elected in 1944. Saskatchewan Teachers' Federation president, four years. CCF/NDP MLA, 1944-1971. Youngest cabinet minister in Canada in 1944. Premier, 1961-1964. Leader of Opposition, 1964-1971. Worked with UN Development Programme, Seoul, Korea.

Lokken, Lloyd of Regina.

Longman, Freda K. of Maryfield.

Lovick, L.D. (Dale) of Nanaimo, B.C. Born in Vancouver. Collegiate instructor. NDP MLA since 1986. Author of *Tommy Douglas Speaks* (Oolichan Books, Lantzville, B.C., 1979).

Mackey, Esther (nee Hansen) of Saskatoon.

Mann, Walter B. of Ottawa, Ont. Educator. Frequent CCF provincial and federal candidate in Ottawa area.

Martin, Ray of Edmonton, Alta. Born in Drumheller, Alta. Guidance counsellor. NDP MLA since 1982. Alberta NDP Leader since 1985.

Mason, Herbert L. of Shellbrook.

McKay, Eric B. of Regina. Born in Summerside, P.E.I. Teacher. District Commissioner, Boy Scouts Saskatchewan, 1925-1940. Served in RCAF. CCF MP for Weyburn, 1945-1949.

McKenzie, Russell of Regina.

McKinnon, Eleanor of Regina. Born in Weyburn. Attended Brandon College. Secretary to Tommy Douglas in Regina and Ottawa, 1944-1986.

McLellan, Alex of Nanaimo, B.C.

McLeod, (Thomas) Ian of Calgary, Alta. Born in Saskatoon. Political reporter; public and private radio journalist. Co-author of *Tommy Douglas, The Road to Jerusalem* (Hurtig, Edmonton, 1987).

McLeod, T.H. (Tommy) of Ottawa, Ont. Born in Weyburn. With CCF government, 1944-1952. Former dean of Arts & Sciences, University of Regina, and dean College of Commerce, University of Saskatchewan. Co-author of *Tommy Douglas, The Road to Jerusalem.*

Meakes, Frank (1917-1989). Born on parents' farm at Punnichy. President Lestock Co-op, 1943-1957. CCF/NDP MLA, 1956-1964 & 1967-1975; cabinet minister and Deputy Speaker.

*Miller, Ted & Patty of Nanaimo, B.C.

Morton, Art of Ganges, Salt Spring Island, B.C.

Mundell, Eva (nee McBain) of Hamiota, Man. Born near Strathclair on father's homestead. High school at Shoal Lake. After marriage lived on farm near Moline, later moved to Hamiota. Teacher 28 years. Community volunteer helping seniors.

Myers, Kate of Weyburn. Born in Yorkshire, Eng., to Canada at age six. Teacher, at Haig School for 31 years. Pastoral assistant, United Church.

Nash, Joyce of Nanaimo, B.C. Born in North Battleford. Held executive positions with B.C., Manitoba and federal CCF/NDP. Campaign manager for leaders in Alberta, Manitoba, B.C., Nova Scotia, P.E.I. and for Tommy Douglas. First woman president of Federal NDP.

Oxelgren, Stan of Regina. Born at Tribune. Pioneer grandparents Erickson farmed in Trossachs and Weyburn areas. Employed with retail co-ops at Govan, Craik and Grenfell. President of Regina CCF at age 21. Regina alderman 12 years. Provincial NDP candidate. Department of Co-ops employee since 1972.

Parsons, Berry of La Ronge.

*Paulley, Daisy of Winnipeg, Man.

Pawley, Howard of Selkirk, Man. Born in Brampton, Ont. Teacher. Lawyer. CCF/NDP MLA for 19 years. Cabinet minister in Schreyer government. Leader of Manitoba NDP, 1979-1988. Premier of Manitoba, 1981-1988.

Peyson, Elsa (Mrs. Colvin) of Regina. Born in Trinidad, BWI. To Canada in 1956. Psychiatric nurse, teacher (Montessori method), real estate agent.

Pickford, Brian of Dundurn.

*Plawucki, Frank of Moose Jaw.

Pretty, Gladys of Weyburn.

Ramage, Hugh & Heather of Wawota. Hugh rode cattle train to Winnipeg and Ontario in 1937. Overseas with Canadian Army for five years, then back to home farm. Long-time Canadian Legion and Saskatchewan Farmers' Union member. Hugh and Heather have had 38 foster children, and three of their own.

Rapley, Kenneth of Strathclair, Man.

Robbins, W.A. (Wes) of Saskatoon. Born in Laura. Teacher. Former Federated Co-operatives Ltd. employee; CCF/NDP MLA for Saskatoon, 1964-1967 & 1971-1982, and cabinet minister.

Robertson, Babs of Weyburn.

Robinson, Hugh of Nanaimo, B.C. Electrician. Executive assistant to Hon. Dave Stupich in Barrett NDP government.

Robinson, Marguerite of Nanaimo, B.C. Alberta native. Thirty years in Party's service in Nanaimo offices of Tommy Douglas and Dave Stupich.

Romanow, Roy of Saskatoon. Born in Saskatoon. Lawyer. CCF/NDP MLA, 1957-1982 & 1986-. Former Attorney General, Deputy Premier. Leader of the Saskatchewan NDP and Opposition Leader.

Roth, Dr. Burns of Toronto, Ont. Ontario native. Practiced medicine in B.C., Yukon. Director of Hospital Administration, Saskatchewan CCF government, 1950-1962.

Sannerud, Evelyn of Medstead.

Schreiner, John R. (Jack) of Vancouver, B.C. Born on Indian Head farm. Former reporter with Regina *Leader-Post*. President, York South (Ont.) NDP Association in 1964. With *Financial Post* since 1973 in Toronto, Montreal; at present, Western Editor, Vancouver. Author, *Transportation* (1980), *The World of Canadian Wine* (1984), *The Refiners, A History of B.C. Sugar* (1989).

Schubert, Chris of Winnipeg, Man. Farmed south of Dafoe. Retired. International representative with Retail Wholesale and Department Store Union; RWDSU vice-president, 1958-1970. Winner of Lucille Ono Pioneer Award, Manitoba NDP.

Scotton, Cliff of Nanaimo, B.C. Born in London, Eng. British Labour Party member. Member of Parliament Press Gallery, Ottawa, for five years. Former editor of *Canadian Labour*. Worked for CCF/NDP in Ontario, B.C. and Manitoba; longest serving Federal Secretary. In 150 election campaigns.

Sears, Robin of Toronto, Ont.

Shoyama, T.K. (Tommy) of Victoria, B.C. Born in Kamloops, B.C. Father emigrated from Japan in 1898. Interned with family during World War II. Edited paper for Japanese Canadians. Served with Canadian Army Intelligence. Economic advisor to Saskatchewan government, 1946-1962. In federal government service, 1964-1979; deputy minister of two departments. Visiting professor, University of Victoria,

Sigurdson, Tom of Edmonton, Alta. Born in Vancouver, B.C. Organizer for Alberta NDP; executive assistant to late Grant Notley; NDP MLA since 1986.

Sinclair, Don of Victoria, B.C. Born in Edinburgh, Scotland. To Canada at age 16 with father to farm south of Avonlea. Forty years with Saskatchewan Wheat Pool in construction department, as agent, field man and assistant secretary. Witnessed Regina Riot in 1935. Overseas World War II (commando operation). NDP federal candidate, 1965.

Smishek, Walter E. of Regina. Born in Poland, to Canada at age five. Former executive secretary, Saskatchewan Federation of Labour; staff member, Retail Wholesale and Department Store union. Former NDP MLA, 1964-1982, cabinet minister.

*Smith, Foster of Shoal Lake, Man.

*Smith, Mrs. Olive of Regina.

Snyder, Gordon of Moose Jaw. Born in Moose Jaw. Former CPR locomotive engineer; Bombardier, RCAF; operator of family farm; CCF/NDP MLA, 1960-1982, and cabinet minister.

*Sorrell, Bernice of Weyburn.

Stade, Rev. Armand D. of Regina. Born in Elmwood, Ont. To North Battleford when very young. CCF candidate in 1935 (Maple Creek). Superintendent for Home Missions, United Church.

Struthers, J.A.C. (Jim) of Regina. Longtime CCF/NDP member. Free lance writer and publisher. Worked with government of Saskatchewan, Sherwood Co-op and Credit Union. Regina travel agent.

Stupich, Dave of Nanaimo, B.C. Chartered accountant. Flying instructor World War II. Past president, B.C. NDP. Former CCF/NDP MLA, first elected in 1963, re-elected six times. Cabinet minister in Barrett NDP government. MP since 1988.

Tamaki, T.K. (Tom) of Regina. Born in Vancouver. Interned with family during World War II. Lawyer. Joined CCF government in 1953. Former Associate Deputy Minister, Department of Mineral Resources, Saskatchewan NDP government.

Tansley, Don of Ottawa, Ont. Born in Regina. Army service Overseas. Former chairman, Medical Care Commission in Saskatchewan CCF government.

Taylor, Alex of Regina. Born in Glasgow, Scotland. Grew up in Toronto. United Church minister, Eatonia, 1965-1971. Former NDP MLA, 1971-1975, cabinet minister. Minister, Zion United Church.

Thomas, Margaret (nee Telford) of Regina. Born in Yorkton. After university worked for CCF Caucus in Ottawa and for federal CCF secretary, David Lewis. Assisted her husband, Lewis H. Thomas, with manuscripts of his books including *The Making of a Socialist, The Recollections of T.C. Douglas* (University of Alberta Press, 1982).

Thurston, Cliff of Regina. Born in Drinkwater. Family farm now part of northwest Regina. Former CCF/NDP MLA, 1956-1964, party whip; vice-president, Saskatchewan CCF.

Trehas, Luetta (nee Dosman) of Regina. Born in Tompkins to pioneer parents. Former teacher; poet, author of *Buffalo Bean Stories* (1980).

Tufford, Audrey of Portage la Prairie, Man. Teacher and farmer. Long-time CCF/NDP member: constituency president, councillor, candidate.

Valecourt, Janice of Ladysmith, B.C. Lived in Regina and Winnipeg. Grandfather Ted Hargreaves of Ernfold drove Tommy Douglas during election campaigns in the 1930s.

Walker, Harvey G. of North Battleford. Barrister and solicitor.

Walker, R.A. (Bob) (1916-1989). Born in Regina. Teacher, Co-op manager, served with RCAF, lawyer, farmer. CCF/NDP MLA, 1948 -1967; Attorney General.

Wallace, Barbara (nee Brookman) of Nanaimo, B.C. Born in Coronation, Alta. Secretary to Colin Cameron when he was MLA. Former NDP MLA, 1975-1986.

Walter, Alice of Weyburn. Farm wife. Active in Weyburn Co-op, Credit Union, Wheat Pool, Baptist Church, Horticulture Society.

Wells, Carl N. of Tuxford. Born near Webb to pioneer parents. Overseas for four years, World War II. Farmer. Former director, Federated Co-operatives Ltd. Former board member, Moose Jaw Co-op, school and church boards. NDP federal candidate, 1962.

Wells, Olive E. of Tuxford. Born in Tuxford of pioneer parents. Teacher. CCF organizer; took part in the Prince Albert campaign which defeated Mackenzie King in 1945. The Talbot Farm (Olive and Carl's farm), the homestead of her parents, was selected as a "typical Saskatchewan farm" for the visit of HRH Queen Elizabeth and Prince Philip in 1959.

Whelan-Enns, Gaile of Aubigny, Man. Born in Regina. Has worked as director of Regina Co-ordinated Youth Services, public relations director for Globe Theatre, Regina; tour director for Prairie Theatre Exchange of Winnipeg; chief researcher for the Manitoba award winning history, *Gretna, Window on the Northwest* (1987). Editor, Manitoba *New Democrat*. Communications co-ordinator, Manitoba NDP.

Williams, Clarence B. of Windsor, Ont. Left Tisdale in early 1940s. Former auto worker. Long-time union and CCF/NDP activist. CCF provincial candidate, 1959.

Wilson, Ian J. of Saskatoon. New Zealand native who came to Saskatchewan during World War II. Former Deputy Minister, Department of Education; first principal of Kelsey Institute, Saskatoon; former chairman, Saskatchewan Legal Aid Commission.

Wooff, R.H. (Bob) of Turtleford. Born in Yorkshire, Eng. To Canada in 1906. Farmer; Wheat Pool committee member for 26 years. Former CCF/NDP MLA: 1944-1948, 1952-1956, 1964-1971. Author of *Following the Gleam* (1980) and *Early History of the CCF in the Turtleford Constituency* (1985).

*Yeaman, Al of Weyburn.

The Authors

Ed (Edward Charles) Whelan was born on a farm near Amherstburg, Ontario. He worked in the auto shops in Windsor before coming to Saskatchewan in 1946. Previously he worked during harvest at High River, Alberta, and Tribune, Saskatchewan. He was field man with the Co-operative Union of Saskatchewan, and inspector, board member and chairman of the Provincial Mediation Board, Department of the Attorney General. His experience with the Co-op Union and Mediation Board gave Ed a wide knowledge of the Province. He served on Sherwood Co-op and Credit Union boards and as secretary of the Regina Labour Council. He was elected MLA for Regina City in 1960, re-elected five times, joined the Cabinet in 1975 and left public office in 1979.

In the CCF/NDP, Ed held a variety of offices including Provincial Councillor 1948-1960, and ten years on the Provincial Executive representing Caucus. He has been a regular delegate to provincial and federal conventions. At the present time he is a constituency executive member and Provincial Councillor, and on the board of the CCFund.

Ed's association with Tommy Douglas began in Provincial Council, continued in the Legislature and was maintained by correspondence and visits after Tommy left Regina.

Elizabeth Pemrose Whelan (nee Henry) was born on her parents' homestead in the RM of Shamrock #134 and grew up in Shamrock, Saskatchewan. She was an essay winner in the Saskatchewan Wheat Pool contest of 1933. She was employed by Saskatchewan Pool Elevators and the Co-operative Union of Saskatchewan. For eleven years her column "Short Shots" appeared in *The Commonwealth*. She served as vice-president of the Saskatchewan CCF for five years and during the same period was chairman of the provincial and federal Women's Committees. She appeared before the 1968 Royal Commission on the Status of Women.

With a B.A. in History (University of Regina, 1975) she has worked on projects related to the CCF/NDP including locating surviving delegates from the 1933 CCF convention in Regina who were honoured at the 50th anniversary convention in Regina in 1983; research assistant to C.M. Fines for *The Impossible Dream* (1982); and research for the National Film Board's *Tommy Douglas, Keeper of the Flame*.

TAPED INTERVIEWS ☯

Eldon Anderson interviewed: W.G. (Bill) Davies, Beth Johnson, Eric B. McKay, Russ McKenzie.

George Hoffman interviewed: Roy Coleman, Leroy Durst, Babs Robertson.

Jean Larmour interviewed: Murray Fines, Christena Fox, Gladys Pretty, Bernice Sorrell, Margaret (nee Telford) Thomas.

Jean Larmour/SAB Interviews: With T.C. Douglas and some of his colleagues in the Saskatchewan government, Les Benjamin, Allan E. Blakeney, George R. Bothwell, Marjorie Cooper Hunt, C.M. Fines, T.S. (Tim) Lee, Eleanor McKinnon, T.H. (Tommy) McLeod, J.L. Phelps, Dr. Burns Roth, Don Tansley, R.A. (Bob) Walker.

Ed Whelan interviewed: John H. Archer, B.N. (Barney) Arnason, Tom & Mary Banda, Pam Barrett, Eva Bethel, George R. Bothwell, Ed Broadbent, Percy Brown, E. John Cannon, R.A. Cugnet, Helen Davidson, Ed Finn, Joe Fox, Fr. Isidore Gorski, Mike Harcourt, John Kowalchuk, Eiling Kramer, Alex McLellan, T.H. (Tommy) McLeod, Walter B. Mann, Art Morton, Joyce Nash, Stan Oxelgren, Howard Pawley, Elsa Peyson, Hugh Robinson, Marguerite Robinson, Roy Romanow, Cliff Scotton, T.K. (Tommy) Shoyama, Don Sinclair, Walter E. Smishek, Rev. Armand D. Stade, T.S. (Tom) Tamaki, Alex Taylor, Cliff Thurston, Janice Valecourt, Barbara Wallace.

Pemrose Whelan interviewed: Hugh Alexander, Marvin & Dorothy Bix, Lorraine Boyle, Isabelle Butters, Kate Myers, Alice Walter.

PRINT ✂, FILM & ARCHIVAL SOURCES

Brittain, Donald. *Tommy Douglas, Keeper of the Flame*, National Film Board, 1987. Directed by Elise Swerhone. Written and Narrated by Donald Brittain.

Callwood, June. *The Globe and Mail* (Toronto), Feb. 24, 1988.

Crowe, Jean Margaret. *The Canadian Forum* (Toronto), Nov. 1986.

Curry, D.S. Quoted by Ernie Mutimer, *Saskatchewan Report*, July 1986.

Douglas Papers, SAB.

French, Doris (Shackleton). *The Citizen* (Ottawa), Mar. 1, 1986. (Author of *Tommy Douglas, A Biography*, 1975).

Hugli, Bill. Interviewed by Ed Schroeder, "Living the life of Tommy Douglas helps actor grow," *The Leader-Post* (Regina), Oct. 8, 1986.

Hutchison, Bruce. *Maclean's Magazine* (Toronto), Aug. 1, 1944.

Johnson, Paul. Editor, *The Oxford Book of Political Anecdotes* (1986).

King, Carlyle. From *A Tribute to Tommy* published by the Saskatchewan NDP, Apr. 1986 following the Mar. 18, 1986 memorial service at the Centre of the Arts, Regina.

Leonard, William. S.G.E.A. *The Dome* (Regina), Jan.-Feb. 1962.

Lloyd, Woodrow S. *The Leader-Post* (Regina), Nov. 8, 1961.

Mackenzie King Diaries. University of Toronto Press, 1980.

Manitoba *Commonwealth* (Winnipeg), May 10, 1947.

Maxwell, Grant. *Compass 88* (Toronto).

McKay, J.F. Saskatchewan *Commonwealth* (Regina), Apr. 14, 1971.

Mutimer, Ernie. *Saskatchewan Report Magazine* (Saskatoon), July 1986.

Pocock, Archbishop Philip. Interviewed by Dennis Gruending, *The Prairie Messenger* (Muenster, Sask.), Sept. 25, 1983.

Saskatchewan, *Legislative Debates*, March 18, 1986 (p.85).

Steeves, Dorothy G. *The Compassionate Rebel. Ernest Winch and the Growth of Socialism in Western Canada*, 1960.

Stinson, Lloyd. *Winnipeg Free Press*, Oct. 21, 1976.

Sutherland, Kiefer. Interviewed by Jamie Portman, Southam News. *Star Phoenix* (Saskatoon), Sept. 6, 1988.

Turner, Arthur. *Credit Union Way* (Regina), Nov. 1983.

PHOTO CREDITS

Barrett, Pam: back cover
Boyle, Lorraine Butters: 10
Brockelbank, John E. & Ina: 33
Canapress: 111, 112, 115 (with *Province*), 116, 118 (with *Province*), 121, 132
Davies, W.G.: 81
Douglas, Irma: 5, 6, 9, 15, 19, 31, 34, 49, 120, 131 (top)
Harcourt, Mike: back cover
Knowles, Stanley: 2
Leader-Post **(Regina)**: 57, 78 (Don Healy), 98, 106, 110
Mitchell, June Cooper: 55
Mundell, Eva: 3
Murray Mosher/CALM: 125, 128
Nanaimo-Cowichan-The Islands NDP: 114
National Archives of Canada/Public Archives of Canada: 44, 66, 85 (top)
National Film Board/SAB: 72
NDP, Federal: 84, 89, 93, 103, 123
NDP, Manitoba: 95, 126
Oxelgren, Stan: 47, 131 (bottom)
Paulley, Daisy: 101
Romanow, Roy: back cover
Saskatchewan Archives Board: 13, 17, 24, 26, 27, 28, 30, 32, 35, 36, 38, 39, 40, 41, 43, 48, 53, 54, 58, 60, 62, 73, 74, 76, 80, 82, 86, 90
Saskatchewan *Commonwealth*: Broadbent, back cover
Saskatchewan Wheat Pool/SAB: 8
Smishek, Walter E.: 102
Snyder, Gordon: 129
Soo Line Historical Museum, Weyburn: 22
Stupich, Dave: 109, 117
T.C. Douglas Calvary Centre, Weyburn: 14, 21
Wallace, Barbara: 107, 108, 113
Western Canada Pictorial Index/Carberry Plains Museum: 4
WCPI/Manitoba NDP: 96
WCPI/Oblate Brothers Collection: 77
Weyburn *Review*: 69, 71, 104, 122, 124
Whelan, Ed & Pemrose: 25, 37, 46, 68, 85 (bottom), 91, 94